BRAIN-COMPATIBLE MATHEMATICS

Diane L. Ronis

SkyLight
Professional
Development

Arlington Heights, Illinois

Brain-Compatible Mathematics

Published by SkyLight Professional Development
2626 S. Clearbrook Dr., Arlington Heights, IL 60005
800-348-4474 or 847-290-6600
Fax 847-290-6609
info@skylightedu.com
http://www.skylightedu.com

Senior Vice President, Product Development: Robin Fogarty
Director, Product Development: Ela Aktay
Acquisitions Editor: Jean Ward
Project Coordinator: Amy Kinsman
Editor: Stuart Hoffman
Cover Designer and Illustrator: David Stockman
Book Designer: Bruce Leckie
Production Supervisor: Bob Crump
Proofreader: Jodi Keller
Indexer: Candice Cummins Sunseri

LCCCN 98-61808
ISBN 1-57517-150-3

2387V
Item Number 1712
Z Y X W V U T S R Q P O N M L K J I H G F E D C
08 07 06 05 04 03 02 01 00   15 14 13 12 11 10 9 8 7 6 5 4 3

For all my fellow teachers struggling
to give their students the best of
themselves . . . this book is for them.

CONTENTS

SECTION II
SAMPLE UNIT TASKS

FOREWORD

I was recently working with a group of fifth grade teachers who were struggling with the question of how to help their students perform better for the state tests. Since the new state tests require a student to do more than operations and computations, the teachers were faced with a serious problem: How would they teach students better problem solving skills? In addition, the state required that students justify their reasoning process in relation to getting the answer to the problem. In other words, students were going to have to apply what they were learning and be thoughtful about their procedures.

As we discussed possible instructional strategies, one teacher suddenly had an insight, "You mean that I will have to give as much time to teaching mathematics as I have been giving for reading and writing?" Another instantly added, " I guess we will have to think about this as we do the writing process. We will need to know when to do mini lessons, provide problem solving time, and how to integrate the math with our other core subjects."

Voila—Diane Ronis' book that provides theory and practice. She carefully grounds her pedagogy in the current understanding of how the brain operates and multiple intelligences. She then provides rich classroom examples with management tools to move teachers immediately into practice. I wish I had her book when I was meeting with those fifth grade teachers!

We are all confronted with the enormous pressures that our new learning standards have placed on us. We can no longer be satisfied with the fact that students are able to compute. We are now asking the far more complex question: How can they show us what they can do when they are faced with a situation in which they are uncertain exactly what to do? This question, although more difficult to measure, is all about the life-long learning skills we desire for children growing up in an age of information.

x

In this information age, our populace will need to be able to understand statistics, probability, read graphs, and fundamentally have a much greater mathematical literacy than we previously required. This book helps us make a transition from a forty-five minute math period to developing students who can think mathematically.

BENA KALLICK

PREFACE

This book has been part of my dream for a long time. I began designing brain-compatible project units when I first started teaching mathematics at the middle school level. I knew that if I was bored with textbook-style worksheets and rote learning, my students must have been even more miserable. In an attempt to make the learning more enjoyable, I tried to make it more interesting, more relevant, and more open-ended. What I did not expect was the quantum leap in the level of student growth that occurred with this nontraditional methodology.

I became fascinated with the revolutionary work that was then occurring in the field of brain research, since that new data appeared to be so compatible with my own teaching philosophy. As I researched the topic in depth during my doctoral studies, I found that all I had done intuitively was now justified and legitimized through scientific research. There was hard scientific evidence to explain why my students were so captivated by and experienced such success with the units I designed. This work has been a labor of love, a vision and a passion which has grown out of my personal joys and frustrations in the classroom. It was so well-received by students, parents, and administrators, that I wanted to share its success with other teachers as well.

I have found that many of the project and portfolio books currently in circulation are oversimplified and lack background and purpose. My desire is to create a book innovative educators can use with comfort and ease . . . one that gives them the knowledge and rationale for those vital changes now taking place in education . . . a book that can help them make the transition more easily into the new instruction/assessment paradigm.

It is my hope that this book helps them do just that.

INTRODUCTION

After many years of teaching, I have finally found the reason for my students' continued success and fascination with authentic project units. Recent brain research points to the fact that the human brain innately seeks to make meaning from and find relevance in its surroundings.

Through relevant and meaningful learning, students are able to painlessly "absorb" knowledge rather than struggle with its acquisition. The positive interdependence between the learner's natural curiosity and search for meaning, and the project-based method of instruction can be demonstrated by the fact that the intrinsic reward of a job well done motivates the students far beyond any extrinsic reward previously offered. Natural curiosity was the motivation for my students—the desire to see what "the results would show."

This book has been designed to make the implementation of a brain-compatible, project-unit approach to mathematics instruction readily available to teachers of all grade and ability levels.

Section 1 comprises seven chapters covering the background of and rationale for brain-compatible learning, including such topics as performance-based instruction and assessment, performance-task development, multiple intelligences theory, brain-based instruction and problem-solving strategies, as well as rubrics, portfolios, and other assessments for those strategies.

Section 2 has portfolio-ready sample unit project tasks complete with instruction outlines, evaluations, and rubrics for teachers as well as students, in addition to the student reflection guides. These project tasks are divided into three levels: primary and elementary, elementary and middle, and secondary.

At the back of the book you will find a glossary and a list of references.

Enormous strides have been made in the field of mathematics education since the National Council of Teachers of Mathematics (NCTM) Standards document was first published in 1989. The results from the Third International Mathematics and Science Study (TIMSS) only serve to emphasize that there is still much to do for this paradigm shift to be complete. This book is about making that shift easier for the classroom teacher already overloaded with demands from students, parents, administrators, and school districts. I hope that this guide will make the teacher's role more enjoyable, and the students' role more successful.

SkyLight Training and Publishing Inc.

SECTION I

FOUNDATIONS OF BRAIN-COMPATIBLE LEARNING

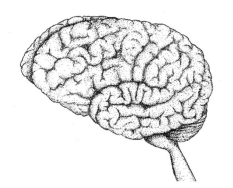

INTRODUCTION

How Can We Change Instruction to Make It More Brain-Compatible?

Performance-based learning is an instructional methodology that makes use of the recent research into brain function, and the implications of this research for education. It focuses on not only the manner in which students gain knowledge, understanding, and proficiency, but also the manner in which students demonstrate these skills.

Recent research into brain physiology and function is providing a newer understanding of how humans learn by helping us redefine our concept of intelligence. These investigations have revealed that our established methods of educating children inhibit rather than encourage their learning. By discouraging, ignoring, or working against the natural learning processes of the brain, our traditional didactic methodologies appear to hinder rather than help the brain learn.

To explain it in simple terms, the brain consists of three major blocks: the brain stem, the limbic system, and the cortex. While the brain stem controls life functions such as breathing and heartbeat, the limbic system serves as the seat of emotion, and the cortex contains the neural networks that result in our capacity for logic and reason. Scientists divide the cortex into four areas called lobes: occipital, frontal, parietal, and temporal.

The occipital lobe, in the rear of the brain, is responsible for vision, while the frontal lobe is involved with problem solving and creativity. The parietal lobe (located in the top area) processes the higher thinking skills and language functions. The temporal lobes (left and right sides) are primarily responsible for hearing, memory, meaning, and language. There is overlap in the functions of these lobes since the entire brain works as an integrated unit. The area in the middle of the brain includes the hippocampus, thalamus, hypothalamus, and amygdala. This midbrain area is also known as the limbic system.

HOW CAN WE CHANGE INSTRUCTION TO MAKE IT MORE BRAIN-COMPATIBLE?

3

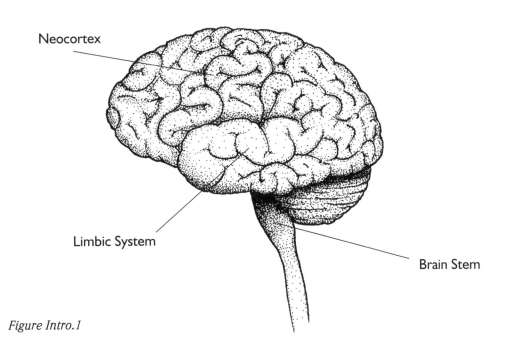

Neocortex

Limbic System

Brain Stem

Figure Intro.1

From *Brain-Compatible Classrooms,* by Robin Fogarty. © 1997 by SkyLight Training and Publishing, Inc. Reprinted with permission of SkyLight Training and Publishing Inc., Arlington Heights, IL.

The brain stem, limbic system, and cortex (see Figure Intro.1) all work through an electromagnetic process which distributes both chemicals and electrical charges through a network of connections extending throughout the brain and body. Recent research has revealed that the process of learning begins with the growth of additional neural connections stimulated by the passage of electrical current along nerve cells (neurons) and is then enhanced by chemicals (neurotransmitters) discharged into the spaces between neighboring cells (synapses). Each time a particular pathway is used, additional connections are created that ease the future use of those same neurons.

If learning is the development of connections between neural networks, then the question is whether we can enhance such growth through education. The notable theorist Davis Perkins has advanced the theory that there are three different kinds of intelligence: neural, experiential, and reflective. We receive neural intelligence at birth. The networks established at birth may vary from person to person, giving some individuals the capacity to process incoming signals more quickly or with more discrimination than others. The second and third intelligences, experiential and reflective, are more malleable and can be changed and developed. Perkins suggests that life experiences cause new neural connections to develop, and as we reflect on our behaviors and past experiences, we find alternative paths, and make new connections. In other words, it is the strengthening of neural pathways through varied and different kinds of instruction and practice that allows us to make connections to prior knowledge which then, in turn, allows for comprehension and learning to occur.

While Howard Gardner's theory of multiple intelligences might follow a somewhat different train of thought, it is not inconsistent with the work of Perkins. Gardner postulates that while the current eight intelligences he identifies (linguistic, logical-mathematical, spatial, kinesthetic, musical, interpersonal, intrapersonal, and naturalist) exist at different levels in the neural networks of individuals at birth, they can be enhanced through experience and reflection.

The work of Hart, Caine and Caine, and others, which examines the brain's propensities for information seeking, processing, and organizing, suggests that in order to capitalize on these propensities, instruction and information must be organized so as to be more brain-compatible. Since the role of emotion is also intrinsic to learning, strategies for its inclusion are an additional component to these theories. The more meaning an experience has for a learner, the more that learner becomes emotionally involved in the experience. In this way "meaningfulness" becomes the prime motivator in the learning process.

Three conditions are necessary for brain-compatible learning to occur. The first is "orchestrated immersion," where the learning environments are set up so that the students can be fully immersed in the learning experience. The second, "relaxed alertness," refers to the concentrated effort to eliminate fear from the learning environment while at the same time maintaining a high level of intellectual challenge. The third condition, that of "active processing," describes a situation where the learner is given time to consolidate and internalize information through the physical and mental processing of that information.

Caine and Caine (1994) believe that the mental, emotional, and physical health of an individual must be assured before an optimum state of learning is possible. A perceived threat to any of these factors results in a "downshifting," a reaction that causes changes to occur in both the brain and the body.

HOW CAN WE CHANGE INSTRUCTION TO MAKE IT MORE BRAIN-COMPATIBLE?

5

It is this downshifting that causes us to redden with embarrassment, feel our palms become clammy, and even freeze momentarily when we have to perform before an audience. When we downshift, we limit our ability to focus and think in complex and creative ways. This also explains why some of us perform poorly in pressure or exam situations. To counter such downshifting and allow for a state of "relaxed alertness" in which optimum learning can occur, it is necessary to have a relaxed nervous system and a sense of security (or in teaching terms, a "safe," non-threatening classroom environment that values risk taking).

The kinds of learning activities that are most effective are those that are compatible with the way the brain works. As teachers, we need to help students have appropriate experiences as well as help them to capitalize on those experiences. By taking on a new, more complex role than that of "information provider," teachers can help students become more responsible for their own learning.

Much in the way a conductor leads the orchestra, a teacher must now orchestrate the immersion of the learner in complex, interactive experiences that are both rich as well as authentic. Work must be presented in a way that is both challenging and meaningful to the students and that will elicit the intrinsic motivation identified as realized alertness. Intensive metacognition and analysis must take place for the learner to develop insight into the problem, about possible strategies and methods of approaching the problem, and about learning in general (the processing of the experience).

Recent brain research has led to implications based on new levels of knowledge and insight regarding teaching and learning. These educational implications appear to emphasize the following factors:

- Children learn in a variety of different ways.
- Students do best when they actively participate in the learning.
- Children need to make connections not only intellectually, but also physically and emotionally with the topics they are studying.
- Feedback between student and teacher helps to fine-tune the brain's patterns and programs.
- For maximum learning, students must feel safe and secure.

Renate and Geoffrey Caine (1994) offer some of the following recommendations for the implementation of brain-based learning in schools:

1. Provide variety in the methods of instruction and types of classroom stimulation, for example, project units, field trips, speakers, varied and different media.

2. Have students actively create products and make presentations or exhibitions using their interests as a springboard for the project concepts.

3. Create individualized learning plans with students, tailored to their various learning styles and multiple intelligences as well as their strengths, interests, emotions, and needs.

4. Integrate a cross section of human services to meet student and family needs.

5. Use the community as a resource for learning. Involve students in experiences such as service learning or peer tutoring.

6. Have the teacher act as facilitator, coach, arranger, expediter, stage manager, etc.

7. Ensure that every student has a personal link in school, an advocate or a friend.

The concept of brain-compatible learning leads to new implications for the design of curriculum, instruction, and assessment. In the area of curriculum, contextual learning needs to be designed around student interests and must also engage student emotions. In the area of instruction, students need to work and learn in teams, as well as in a "safe" classroom environment, free of stress and threats. Instruction needs to include stimulating choices as well as physical activity and should make use of peripheral learning. The learning needs to be structured around "real" problems. Learning settings need to be established both outside and inside the classroom. Assessment needs to include an understanding of each individual's learning style and preference, and students must be encouraged to monitor and maximize their learning.

There are parallels between how educators approach teaching and how artists approach their craft. Educators need to be artists in the way they design brain-friendly environments. The most effective way to learn is not by being a passive listener, but by being an active participant in realistic problem-solving experiences occuring in environments where new and innovative ideas are encouraged.

HOW CAN WE CHANGE INSTRUCTION TO MAKE IT MORE BRAIN-COMPATIBLE?

7

For the past 10 years, the National Council of Teachers of Mathematics (NCTM) has been recommending that schools and educators shift their emphasis away from traditional paper-and-pencil tests, and instead, emphasize opportunities for demonstration of mathematical comprehension "through a variety of methods, including portfolios, discussions, presentations, and projects."

While basic knowledge and skills provide an important educational foundation, such "basics" must not become an end in and of themselves. Rather, they should be considered "tools" that enable students to thoughtfully apply knowledge and skills within a meaningful "real-life" context.

Norm-referenced and standardized tests have traditionally provided the basis for comparisons of different populations of students, different educational programs, and even the effectiveness of entire educational systems. For such comparisons, these tests do provide valid and reliable data. However, for an accurate profile of individual students or the manner in which these students accumulate knowledge and understanding, they will always fall short of the mark.

Good and accurate assessment is more than a standardized test grade. It is an integral part of the learning process, and as such, also brings attention to any weakness that may exist within the instruction. Assessment and instruction are so closely interrelated that one cannot successfully function without the other. Ideally, assessment occurs before, during, and after instruction so as to refine lessons to better meet student needs. After a while, instruction and assessment become so well integrated that they are virtually indistinguishable. Performance-based instruction takes this integration to an even higher level. With this type of instruction, the manner in which students will demonstrate the intended knowledge, understanding, and proficiency must also be clearly outlined.

When setting performance criteria (or targets), educators need to keep in mind that the development of student understanding must be one of the primary goals of instruction (understanding is defined here as the ability to apply facts, concepts, and skills appropriately in new situations). Teachers who establish and communicate clear performance goals also recognize that student attitudes and perceptions toward learning are influenced by the extent to which they understand what the expectations are, and what the rationale is behind the use of the instructional activities. Clearly stated performance goals also help to identify curriculum priorities, which in turn enable us to focus effectively on knowledge that is critical and essential.

By the establishment of clear performance criteria, and teaching for understanding, the synthesis of curriculum, instruction, and assessment can best occur. A performance-based philosophy is one in which curriculum is not thought of as simply content to be covered, but rather as desired performances of understanding. When teachers design learning goals and objectives as performance applications requiring demonstration of student understanding, those performance assessments become the targets for teaching and learning, as well as the evidence of understanding and application.

For a performance-based educational program to be effective, it must

- establish clear performance criteria (targets),
- emphasize "authentic" work using "real-life" problems employing the application of knowledge and skills,
- result in a tangible product or performance,
- employ multiple or "messy" approaches and solutions rather than a single, "neat" answer (the way things happen outside the classroom),
- stress self-reflection and self-evaluation,
- value the learning process itself by including works-in-progress,
- reflect good instructional practices grounded in student feedback and teacher revision,
- encourage critical thinking skills, rather than mere rote memorization, and
- demonstrate what students can do, rather than what they cannot do.

Section 1 of this book focuses on recent brain research findings that have led to brain learning principles such as the innate search for meaning and the uniqueness of each individual. It is through these principles that a scientific basis for performance-based instruction and assessment, problem-based learning, and multiple intelligences is being established. These brain-based principles and educational theories are then are implemented in section 2 of the book through original, ready-to-use project unit tasks containing metacognitive activities as well as brain-based mathematics activities and projects. These project units and tasks are designed so that (a) learning is structured around "real" problems that engage students' interests and emotions, (b) students work and learn in teams, (c) instruction includes stimulat-

HOW CAN WE CHANGE INSTRUCTION TO MAKE IT MORE BRAIN-COMPATIBLE?

9

ing choices as well as physical activity, (e) assessment includes an understanding of each student's learning style and preference, and (f) students monitor as well as maximize their own learning. All project units, performance tasks, individual and group evaluations, rubrics, and reflections have been classroom-tested and specifically designed for easy use and implementation. While the book concentrates on the subject area of mathematics, the projects are interdisciplinary.

Each project unit is comprehensive and can either stand alone or be used in conjunction with other units. Each unit contains its own specific set of objectives, vocabulary, and directions for implementation, as well as group and self-evaluation outlines created to be compatible with brain learning principles.

According to Caine and Caine (1997), brain-based classrooms provide the essence of what education needs to become:

> In a school or a classroom practicing brain-based learning, the importance of the different intelligences and learning styles is taken for granted. Assessment includes, but moves beyond, paper/pencil tests for surface knowledge. We expect to see authentic assessments of all types and students participating in the evaluation of their own learning process and progress. . . . In such schools and classrooms, learning is driven by student purposes and meanings; and teachers facilitate and enhance student learning.

CHAPTER 1

PERFORMANCE-BASED LEARNING AND ASSESSMENT

In the act of learning, people obtain content knowledge, acquire skills, and develop work habits—and practice the application of all three to "real-world" situations. Performance-based learning and assessment represent a set of strategies for the acquisition and application of knowledge, skills and work habits through the performance of tasks that are meaningful and engaging to students.

—Educators in Connecticut's Pomperaug Regional School District 15 (1996)

Performance assessment is assessment based on observation and judgment. The evaluator observes a student perform a task or reviews a student-produced product, and then judges the quality of that task or product. While performance tasks can be designed to have students demonstrate their understanding through the application of acquired knowledge to a new and different situation, good performance tasks always involve more than one acceptable solution, often calling for students to explain or defend their solutions. Performance tasks are both an integral part of learning and an opportunity for assessing student performance quality (Stiggins 1994 and McBrien and Brandt 1997).

Assessment and accountability standards have long been quantified through the wide-scale administration of standardized tests. The inherent flaws and limitations of traditional standardized tests are numerous. Test content is usually the result of a negotiated compromise among a team of curriculum "experts." Test publishers ensure that chosen test objectives are matched to widely used textbooks, resulting in the narrowing of the content covered. Test emphasis on basic skills further constrains and limits the complexity of test content. Practical considerations constrain content even more through the use of multiple-choice format, a method that is less expensive and easier to administer than student-generated, open-ended responses.

In spite of these drawbacks, the public continues to give standardized test scores great weight. When these scores have serious consequences such as state financing, student placement, or town ranking, teachers find they must "teach to the test," a practice resulting in the corruption of instruction. Teaching to the test cheapens and undermines the authenticity of the scores as being accurate measures of what students know. It also creates an unbalanced emphasis on tested areas, at the expense of untested areas. For example, teachers often find they must discard essay-type tests since those kinds of tests are inefficient for multiple choice test preparation. The most efficient type of instruction for the multiple-choice format is instruction that consists of drill and practice on isolated, decontextualized skills.

In the society of twenty years ago, standardized tests seemed to serve as reasonable indicators of student learning. With the current knowledge of how the brain actually does process and acquire new learning, the incompatibility of standardized tests with deeper levels of understanding gives pause for educators, parents, and policy makers to reflect on the likelihood of such tests being inadequate and misleading as measures of achievement or accountability. While they are neither valid nor accurate indicators of actual learning, standardized tests are excellent indicators of fact memorization and test-taking skills.

However, the memorization of bits and pieces of knowledge cannot sufficiently prepare today's youth for the challenges of the next century. Valid tests must require more complex and challenging mental processes from students. The existence of more than one correct approach or response must be acknowledged and encouraged.

Traditional Versus Brain-Friendly Assessments

Assessment should be the central aspect of classroom practice that links curriculum, teaching, and learning. Unfortunately, however, assessment is primarily used by teachers to assign grades at the end of a unit of instruction and to differentiate the successful students from the unsuccessful. Teachers tend to rely heavily on written work involving the completion of imitative exercises and routine problems. This traditional practice stands in sharp contrast to the conception of assessment reflected in the Standards documents of the National Council of Teachers of Mathematics (NCTM) (1989, 1991, 1995). These documents present a vision of assessment that is ongoing and that is carried out in multiple ways: by listening to, observing, and talking with students; by asking students questions to help reveal their reasoning; by examining students' individual or group written and/ or project work.

When conceived of and used in this constructive manner, assessment helps teachers gain better insight into their students' thinking and reasoning abilities. Assessment can also be a powerful tool for enabling

$$4 \times 8 =$$
$$5 \times 8 =$$
$$6 \times 8 =$$
$$7 \times 8 =$$
$$8 \times 8 =$$

teachers to monitor the effectiveness of their own teaching, judge the utility of the learning tasks, and consider where to go next in instruction.

Performance assessments will not work unless educators engage in performance-based classroom instruction as well. In order to achieve consistent performance-based instruction, educators must use performance-based tasks combined with ongoing assessment:

assessment ➔ feedback ➔ instruction modification ➔ assessment ➔ feedback...

Importance of Performance Assessment

Traditional assessments such as multiple-choice and fill-in chapter/unit tests have not done an adequate job of profiling students with validity or accuracy. Rather, what is needed are assessments that

- more closely reflect the learning goals we have for students;
- communicate the right messages to students about what is being valued;
- align with current theories of instruction; and
- describe students rather than sort them out.

Performance assessment has recently come into the forefront, due to the nature of the goals various educational groups have set for students. If these new educational goals are to address the concepts of critical thinking, problem solving, communication, collaborative working, and lifelong learning, then a different, more innovative assessment process is needed for the task of evaluation.

Performance assessment is not a new or novel approach. Educators have always used day-to-day classroom observations of student progress for evaluation purposes. What is new, however, is the attempt to give this evaluation modality a more central role in large-scale assessments, and to make day-to-day evaluation more consistent and systematic. To achieve the goal of making these subjective assessments as objective, systematic, and, therefore, as credible as possible, educators must first be sure that the learning goals are clear. Once these goals have been established, the best assessment technique for each particular goal must be chosen. Performance assessment may or may not always be the best method; it depends on what is being assessed.

Current brain research and cognitive psychology contend that learning occurs when learners construct their own knowledge and develop their own cognitive relationships between concepts and facts. Therefore, in order to become adept at thinking and reasoning, students need to practice solving real problems. Low-achieving students suffer most from a proficiency-driven curriculum. Because schools postpone the practice of higher-order thinking skills instruction until after basic, low-level skills have been mastered, these students are sentenced to dull drill and repetition indefinitely. They never seem to grasp the concepts underlying the drill.

Educators are aware that good instruction actively involves students in the learning process. In the past, having knowledge of large numbers of facts was valued by society; however, with information increasing today at exponential rates, students will be more likely to need the ability to access information and then apply that information to real-life situations. Throughout their lives, today's students will be faced with problems and situations that have no clear-cut correct answers. They will need to analyze those situations and then apply their knowledge and skills to find acceptable solutions. The difficulty, however, is that what students need to know and to be able to do can sometimes be very different from what is being taught in schools. As in the past, students still need to know facts, but the educational emphasis is now shifting.

Traditional assessment formats measure facts and skills in isolation. As the curriculum evolves to better reflect the skills that today's students will need to function effectively in the twenty-first century—skills such as critical thinking, problem solving, and teamwork—the methods of assessing learning must also change. If they do not change, assessment may very well get in the way of reform. If teachers teach to those higher level cognitive skills, yet students continue to be tested on how well they have memorized facts, this obvious conflict of purpose confuses both students and teachers as to what skills society values.

Educators and educational researchers are working to change achievement assessment to better reflect the current educational shift in emphasis, expectations, and standards. This evolving type of assessment, referred to as "alternative assessment," can include a wide variety of assessment formats, in which students create their own responses to questions, rather than choose a response from a given list. Authentic activities involve complex behaviors not easily assessed by traditional paper-and-pencil tests, activities such as (1) the planning and execution of an experiment, (2) the construction of a graph, chart, or diagram, (3) the construction of a scientific or geometric model, or (4) the construction of a concept map (a diagram of the unit concepts [usually shown as circles] and the interrelationships between them [usually drawn as lines connecting two or more concepts]).

Alignment of Curriculum and Assessment

Once the desired educational priorities are established, the focus can then be shifted to the attainment of those priorities. With the goals and instruction practices in place, it is the assessment process that provides a clear understanding as to whether those desired goals have been achieved. If such assessment is not in alignment with the curriculum, then there is no validity to the results achieved, and students get a conflicting message as to what is valued. The alignment of curriculum and assessment must be carefully orchestrated:

> Aligning the curriculum is based on three major decisions: (1) establishing the purposes, outcomes, goals or objectives of the educational enterprise . . .; (2) designing the delivery system by which those goals will be achieved, including instructional design, materials selection, allocation of time and placement of learning; and (3) developing feedback loops for monitoring, collecting evidence of, and evaluating the achievement of our goals as a result of employing that delivery system. (Costa and Kallick 1992)

Sound educational practice dictates that it is the goals of education that must drive the system. New educational goals will form the basis for the everyday skills needed by the citizens of the next millennium. These new educational goals include the development of

- capacity for continued learning,
- knowledge of how to behave when answers to problems are not immediately apparent,
- cooperation and team building,
- precise communication in a variety of modes,
- appreciation for disparate value systems,
- problem solving that requires creativity and ingenuity,
- ability to resolve ambiguous, discrepant, and paradoxical situations,

- generation and organization of an overabundance of technologically produced information,
- pride and craftsmanship of product,
- high self-esteem, and
- personal commitment to larger organizational and global values.

(Costa and Kallick 1992)

Assessment methods must now be changed so as to be consistent with these new goals. Normed-referenced (compared to a set of predetermined standards) standardized test scores result in a static number that reflects the achievement and performance of isolated skills at a specific moment in time. Thinking, however, is dynamic in that we learn from experience, react emotionally to situations, become empowered by problem solving, and are energized by the act of discovery. While educators, policymakers, and the public at large are questioning the value of standardized testing instruments, states are experimenting with and advocating innovative assessment methods such as free-response and open-ended type questions, portfolios, performances, and exhibitions (see below).

These methods are more "authentic" than traditional testing procedures in that

1. they are not neat, contrived little packages, but rather "messy" to solve, having no clear-cut, "single-right-answer" solutions, and are more in keeping with real-life experiences;
2. they allow teachers more leeway in order to diagnose students' abilities with greater accuracy through the observation of student habits and repertoires rather than just recall;
3. they take place during instruction rather than after instruction (as with an end-of-unit test), thereby providing more immediate feedback for teachers to use in the evaluation and modification of the instruction; and
4. they provide timely feedback to the students who through these examples learn from the assessment process itself, and ultimately become the evaluators of their own work.

Educators have long relied on a limited range of assessment measures, primarily traditional pencil-and-paper tests. Assessing goals in the restruc-

18

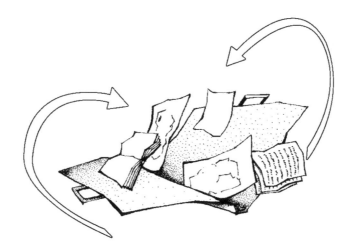

tured school will require an expansion of our repertoire of assessment techniques. Some of the more authentic assessment techniques that provide a more multidimensional perspective of student growth and progress are

- direct observation of student performance in problem-solving situations,
- portfolios of student work developed over time,
- extended projects,
- logs or journals,
- writing samples,
- performance assessment using a set of agreed-upon criteria (a rubric),
- anecdotal records, and
- electronic portfolios (using technology to assist in the collection and recording of student growth over time).

These authentic assessment techniques provide much greater insight into student progress and growth than do traditional paper-and-pencil tests.

Assessment as Continuous Monitoring

Using the recent knowledge gained from brain research and cognitive psychology (how learning occurs), the teacher must continually monitor each student in order to meet the needs of that student. An instructional paradigm such as this is guided by student questions; integrates multiple cultural, racial, and gender values; and is constructivist in that it builds on student biological and experiential prior knowledge. It also supports active experiential learning, fosters collaboration, and takes into account individual learning styles and stages of cognitive development.

Similarly, the role of assessment in the new paradigm must also change. Rather than rewarding only correct responses, assessment must also inquire as to the reasons for obtaining incorrect responses (which, when viewed from the student's perspective, may not be incorrect at all). The role shift emphasizes different kinds of assessment for different purposes, and multiple forms of assessment for determining student learning. Assessment is geared to improving instruction, to stimulating inquiry and personal growth in students, and to fostering cooperative learning. In other words, it must assess what society values; in the educational arena, that is student learning.

Assessment provides the information to power instructional decision making. It is the part of the feedback loop that helps to monitor student progress and make any needed adjustments in instruction. In order to make such adjustments, educators must pay attention to

1. the kinds of student outcomes that monitor progress and emphasize skills such as collaboration, critical thinking, and student ownership of learning;
2. the need for more performance-based assessments that will monitor progress on these new outcomes; and
3. the need for more systematic methods for the gathering and organizing of classroom data and observations.

The integration of assessment and instruction provides the best approach for the continual monitoring of student learning. In its ideal form, this integration is so complete that the lines between assessment and instruction fade. The student is completely unaware of being assessed, of instruction being modified on the spot, or of further cycles of assessment/instruction/ modification of instruction/reassessment and so on. Assessment becomes a continuous activity in the instruction process, designed to create an optimal learning situation for students. It results in an ongoing evaluation and adjustment dynamic on the part of the teacher. To be truly effective, instruction and assessment must be thoroughly integrated. If they aren't, those students who have traditionally performed poorly in the old educational paradigm ("at-risk" students) will be lost in the new one as well.

The NCTM "standards-based" math curriculum materials advocate assessments that

- are embedded within instructional materials,
- use a variety of methods to assess student progress,
- emphasize teacher observation and teacher judgment, and
- provide methods for getting at the reasons behind children's answers.

Viewed in this manner, good assessment becomes more than just an exercise in monitoring at the end of a unit of instruction. It becomes the essential ingredient that forces us to be more clear about what it is we wish to accomplish with our students, and simultaneously, a tool for helping students attain those goals.

Assessment as a Tool for Learning

Both large-scale and classroom assessments influence students directly, for better or worse. Assessment is neither just a neutral collection of information, nor is it merely a way of influencing future instruction by teachers. If designed properly, assessment becomes a way of directly influencing students in a positive manner. Students will learn from doing an assessment activity, since the performance of that activity is in itself an instructional experience. This first-hand experience of the assessment process enables students to develop the skills of self-evaluation.

> We must constantly remind ourselves that the ultimate purpose of evaluation is to have students become self-evaluative. (Costa and Kallick 1992)

Once aligned, curriculum and assessment tools help students to both learn and be assessed using brain-based ideology. The curriculum tools needed for such a shift in framework will be based upon the performance aspect of a learning task, that particular element of the educational equation now requiring a distinctly different methodology for its planning and development.

CHAPTER 2

THE SIX PILLARS OF PERFORMANCE TASK DEVELOPMENT

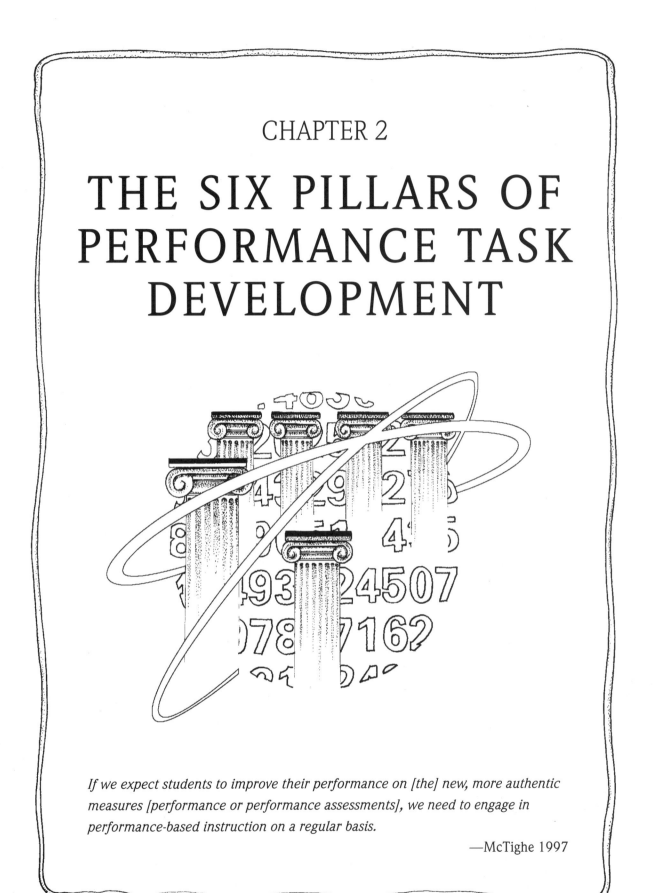

If we expect students to improve their performance on [the] new, more authentic measures [performance or performance assessments], we need to engage in performance-based instruction on a regular basis.

—McTighe 1997

Performance tasks are activities, problems, or projects that require students to demonstrate what they know and can do. These tasks build on earlier content knowledge and process skills, as well as work habits, and are placed in the unit to enhance learning as the students begin to process and synthesize the knowledge and experience gained from that unit. By definition, such tasks cannot be added on at the end of instruction, but instead, are integrated within the unit to enhance and solidify the learning experience. Performance tasks reinforce brain-based learning concepts since they are designed to function much the way the brain learns new information, by introducing new material in an integrated and comprehensive manner rather than as isolated bits and pieces. It is this integration and comprehensiveness that enables the brain to make faster and easier connections.

Performance tasks should be interesting to the students as well as connected to the important content, process skills, and work designs of the curriculum. It is beneficial to have the students take part in the construction of both the task and assessment rubrics, since in this way they are able to develop a sense of ownership of the project and thoroughly understand the assessment standards that will be used in the evaluation.

The Maryland Assessment Consortium, a group of educators involved in developing performance tasks that are tied to district or state standards, has been influential in Maryland's development of criteria, projects, and a philosophy of education grounded in performance-based instruction and assessment. The state recognizes that the manner in which educational improvement occurs is through ongoing performance-based assessment as well as implementation of performance-based instruction. Maryland recommends its teachers use assessments for ongoing feedback, and then adjust their instruction design according to what is needed, throughout the entire learning process.

The development of assessment criteria is complicated since complex tasks cannot be assessed using simple criteria. If an assessment task includes several elements such as a written report, oral presentation, and creative project, each of these elements needs to have its own corresponding set of assessment criteria (evidence of understanding in each category).

The following six basic principles for the establishment of effective performance instruction, as well as steps in good task design and development, are based on the work of Jay McTighe and the Maryland Assessment Consortium.

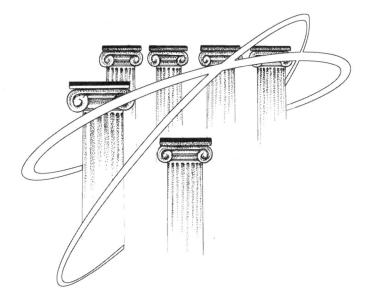

The Six Pillars of Performance Task Development

1. Establish clear performance goals (content standards).
2. Seek to employ "authentic" tasks and products.
3. Teach and emphasize criteria levels and performance standards.
4. Provide models and demonstrations of excellence.
5. Teach strategies explicitly.
6. Use ongoing assessments for feedback and adjustment.

Performance-based instruction is an effective methodology because it allows the teacher to continually monitor for student understanding and be able to then adjust the instruction to clarify and/or eliminate potential areas of confusion and misunderstanding. On the following pages explanations are given for each of the six basic principles that provide the framework for the design, development, and implementation of performance-based learning. Each principle is related to one or more specific steps in task design and development.

24

1. Set Up Clear Performance Goals

PRINCIPLES

- Focus on results (content standards).
- Focus on what students should know and be able to do.
- What is *not* taught is just as important as what *is* taught.
- Concentrate on the critical and essential.
- Concentrate on clear articulation and communication of the performance criteria.

TASKS

- Begin all designs with a clear statement of what is to result: the intended achievement(s) as well as how that achievement will be assessed. (For help in doing this, see Figure 2.1: Sample Problem Ladder Graphic Organizer.)
- Determine those learner goals or content standards that are to be assessed. (What critical and essential outcomes do we want to evaluate?)
- Identify observable and meaningful indicators for each standard (What must students show they know and can do well in order to prove that they understand? How will we know it when we see it?)

What we do not teach is just as important as what we do teach. By being selective in our choices, we are better able to focus the curriculum on the critical and essential skills (those skills our students will need and be able to recall in the future). Educators have often complained of a curriculum that is "a mile wide and an inch deep." One goal of this book is to help educators achieve better student understanding through the avoidance of an overblown curriculum filled with purposeless coverage.

In my first year of teaching middle-level mathematics, I was handed a syllabus with 93 learner outcomes. Since our school year then consisted of a 182-day calendar, I quickly calculated that I would have less than two days per learner outcome, even if I never gave a single test and eliminated all professional days, field trips, and special programs. It was obvious that I would have to hit the ground running in September, and simply teach, test, and move on.

This kind of frustration is not uncommon in the teaching profession. The results of the Third International Mathematics and Science Study (TIMSS) conclusively demonstrated that the mile-wide and inch-deep curriculum

SAMPLE PROBLEM LADDER GRAPHIC ORGANIZER

Curriculum Area(s): _____   Project Length: _____

Performance Task Title: _____   Grade Level(s): _____

Resources/Materials: _____

TASK DESCRIPTION

_____

_____

_____

_____

_____

PROJECT OBJECTIVES

Student comprehension of concepts

- _____
- _____
- _____
- _____

Student skill and process development

- _____
- _____
- _____
- _____

PRODUCTS AND/OR PERFORMANCES

Group Products	Individual Products	Extensions
• _____	• _____	• _____
• _____	• _____	• _____
• _____	• _____	• _____
• _____	• _____	

CRITERIA FOR PRODUCT EVALUATION

Group Products	Individual Products	Extensions
• _____	• _____	• _____
• _____	• _____	• _____
• _____	• _____	• _____
• _____	• _____	

Figure 2.1

results in too little conceptual understanding and weak development of higher-level thinking skills.

In establishing performance goals or targets, two main ideas must be kept in mind:

1. What is it that we want the students to understand?
2. What is it that can demonstrate to us that they do understand? (What kind of assessments ask students to apply and use the new knowledge and/or skills?)

To achieve understanding, we must first think of the curriculum in terms of desired "performances of understanding" (assessments), and then plan backwards so as to focus on the critical and essential knowledge—the knowledge we want our students to retain and be able to recall in the future. Planning backwards simply means organizing the instruction around the content standards and developing assessments that target those content standards. Once the standards (both content and performance standards) have been identified, the choice of assessment evidence can be developed —evidence which demonstrates that the desired learning has been achieved.

In an activity-oriented or authentic curriculum, instruction becomes a means to an end. The question "What instructional purpose will be met by this performance or task?" serves as a guide for developing that task.

2. Employ "Authentic" Project Tasks

PRINCIPLES

"Authentic" refers to tasks that
- have a meaningful real-world context
- use and apply skills as well as knowledge
- are often "messy," with multiple strategies or solutions
- have connections to students' interests and experiences
- serve as a "hook" for engaging students in meaningful learning
- stress student self-reflection and self-evaluation

TASK
- Create a meaningful context for the assessment task based upon real problems and/or student interests.

The term *authentic* refers to real world application(s) of knowledge and skills, as well as connections to student experiences and interests. Authenticity is what helps students see connections between school and the real world. It serves as a hook for engaging students in meaningful and important work.

Authentic tasks that employ the use and application of skills and knowledge are tasks that mimic challenges and problems as they occur in the world outside the classroom. The house-painting project in Chapter 10 of this book is an example of just such an authentic task. The problem as it is posed in the project unit has many possible solutions, none of which offer neat, tidy answers.

The sample units in section 2 of this book are all examples of authentic task projects that have relevancy to the students since they are based on real situations and use a variety of strategies and solutions.

Work is authentic when it

- contains subject content knowledge,
- has meaningful and relevant content (content dealing with issues and problems, themes, or student interests),
- has purpose (enables the students to understand the why in what they are doing),
- has a target audience (identifies an audience to whom the results are directed), and
- results in a tangible product or performance.

Teachers can use the Hierarchy For the Selection and Creation of High-Level Mathematical Tasks (see figure 2.2) as a guide in the selection of performance tasks.

HIERARCHY FOR THE SELECTION AND CREATION OF HIGH-LEVEL MATHEMATICAL TASKS

(Doyle 1988, NCTM 1991, Resnick 1987)

Mathematical Tasks—Higher-Level Demand Tasks:
- require sophisticated and complex non-algorithmic thinking;
- require the ability to regulate one's own cognitive processes;
- require students to access relevant knowledge and make appropriate uses of such knowledge in task completion;
- require students to analyze and actively examine any task constraints that might limit possible strategies and solutions; and
- require considerable cognitive effort, and many result in some level of student stress due to the unpredictable nature of the solution process.

Procedures with Connections—Higher-Level Demand Tasks:
- focus attention on the use of procedures for deeper levels of understanding;
- suggest general and broad procedures that are closely connected to the underlying concepts rather than narrow procedures and rigid algorithms;
- are presented in different ways, so as to address the multiple intelligences; and
- require some degree of cognitive effort in order to connect with the conceptual ideas that underlie the procedures necessary for comprehension and successful task completion.

Procedures Without Connections—Lower-Level Demand Tasks:
- are algorithmic in that the use of the procedure is either specifically called for or is evident from prior instruction;
- have little ambiguity or complexity, and require limited cognitive effort for successful completion;
- have no connection to the broad underlying concepts; and
- are focused on the production of correct answers rather than mathematical connections, understandings, or explanations.

Memorization—Lower-Level Demand Tasks:
- consist of reproducing previously learned rules, definitions, and formulas or memorizing new rules, definitions, and formulas;
- are not complex or ambiguous, and involve only the replication of familiar material; and
- have no connection to the broad underlying concepts.

Figure 2.2

3. Teach and Emphasize Criteria Levels and Performance Standards

PRINCIPLES

A scoring rubric consists of . . .
- a fixed scale (for example, four criteria levels)
- a description of the characteristics for each of the performance standards
- sample responses that illustrate each standard

TASK
- Identify the thinking skills/thought processes that will encourage the thoughtful application of knowledge and skills.

The manner in which the project or task will be assessed, as well as the standards that will be used to assess it, must be clearly explained to the students before beginning the unit. It is best when both teachers and students agree on the criteria to be used for the standards and evaluation. There should be no mystery or guess work on the student's part as to what the basis for the grade will be.

The best way to achieve this is by establishing a rubric (scoring tool) specifically for the purpose of grading. The rubric contains the criteria that categorize the different levels of quality, understanding, or proficiency being used in the assessment.

Knowledge of the rubric will not automatically appear in the minds of the students. They must be carefully instructed with regard to the rubric's elements, so that there is no confusion and the resulting project grade is not a surprise.

It is easier for students to gain an understanding of the rubric if they have input in its design. Through such rubric design the students develop a thorough understanding of what the criteria are as well as how those criteria will be used in the assessment. Chapter 6 discusses rubrics in depth. The rubrics there are general in nature, and can help students visualize the different achievement levels as well as the goal for which they are striving.

4. Provide Models and Demonstrations of Excellence

PRINCIPLES

"If we expect students to do excellent work, they have to know what excellent work looks like." (Dr. Grant Wiggins)

- A benchmark is a standard for judging a performance or a product.
- Benchmarks, used as exemplars (models), demonstrate student work and achievement that highlight the specific characteristics displayed at each of the different levels of the rubric performance scale.

TASKS

- Identify the student product/performance that will provide evidence of attainment of the outcomes/standards and what will provide evidence of understanding (these should be guided by a purpose and an audience).
- Select exemplary responses to activity.
- Construct evaluation scoring tools (rubrics) for each activity.

Explaining the rubric is not enough for comprehension of the different rubric levels. Students must be shown what the different benchmarks (rubric levels) look like. They need to see tangible sample student work at all rubric levels to completely grasp the concepts, internalize the concepts, and, as a result, be able to evaluate their own work in an informed manner. The ability to critique one's own work is a prerequisite for becoming a lifelong learner.

One good method for developing student knowledge of rubric standards is by using a "Benchmark Bulletin Board." During a project unit it is helpful to have on display samples of past student work that illustrates each of the different benchmark levels. The students are free to refer to these examples throughout the unit to see if their work indeed measures up.

5. Teach Strategies Explicitly

PRINCIPLES

- problem-solving heuristics (heuristics are instructive methods that aid learning through exploration)
- self-moderating strategies
- thinking skills processes

- mnemonic techniques (serve as a cueing structure to facilitate recall; for example, acronyms, rhyming, sequence linking)
- study skills
- organizational strategies

TASK

- Identify the criteria which will be used to evaluate student products and performances.

Problem-solving skills and critical thinking competencies must be taught explicitly if the goal is performance improvement. Problem-solving skills, best developed through first-hand experience with real-life problems, entail solutions based on observation, logical thinking, and analysis of sound evidence.

The strategies listed above are all very teachable, and will translate into improved performance results. Good direct instruction includes information about not only what a particular technique is, but how and when to use it.

Chapter 5 deals in depth with problem-solving strategies as well as tips for strategy implementation.

6. Use Ongoing Assessments for Feedback and Adjustments

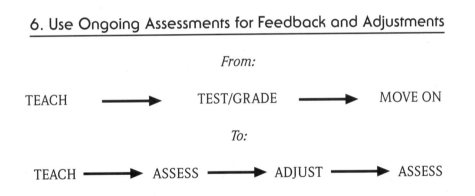

From:

TEACH ➝ TEST/GRADE ➝ MOVE ON

To:

TEACH ➝ ASSESS ➝ ADJUST ➝ ASSESS

Quality is best achieved through consistent, incremental improvement. This refers to the practice of giving regular assessments throughout the unit, followed by necessary adjustments based on the information gained from those assessments. Deeper levels of understanding and higher levels of proficiency are achieved only as a result of trial, practice, adjustments based on feedback, and more practice.

Performance-based instruction underscores the importance of using ongoing assessment to provide guidance for improvement throughout the learning process. The traditional method of waiting until a unit has been completed and then assessing that unit with a separate, unrelated activity called a "test," does not help in the adjustment or the modification of instruction when it is most needed, during the learning process itself.

Brain-Compatible Framework

The framework of the six pillars creates an ensemble of learning, assessment, and performance that is highly brain-compatible. The relevancy of performance tasks fulfills the brain's innate search for meaning. The open-ended nature of these tasks allows for a variety of learning styles and multiple intelligences to flourish, and the low-stress, highly challenging classroom environment encourages the development of the kind of meaningful learning that the brain craves. In this way assessment is transformed into something much more important than the assignment of a grade at the end of a unit. Student performance and assessment become the most relevant part of the curriculum, with substantial influence on the make-up and direction of the instruction.

CHAPTER 3

MULTIPLE INTELLIGENCES AND BRAIN-COMPATIBLE LEARNING

It is of the utmost importance that we recognize and nurture all of the varied human intelligences, and all of the combinations of intelligences. We are all so different largely because we all have different combinations of intelligences. If we recognize this, I think we will have at least a better chance of dealing appropriately with the many problems that we face in the world.

—Gardner 1987

The six pillars of performance task development discussed in the previous chapter provide a basis for the design of tasks using brain-based instruction, assessment, and performance. The open-ended nature of such performance tasks allows for a wide variety of learning styles and multiple intelligences to function symbiotically within the same classroom environment.

Theory of Multiple Intelligences

Any study of learning-style theories would be grossly incomplete without a discussion of Howard Gardner's Theory of Multiple Intelligences. Basically, a person's learning style is Gardner's intelligences put to work; in other words, learning styles are the manifestations of intelligences operating in natural learning contexts. Gardner provided a means of mapping the broad range of human abilities and capabilities by grouping them into eight comprehensive categories or "intelligences":

1. *Linguistic:* the capacity to use words effectively, whether orally or in writing.
2. *Logical-Mathematical:* the capacity to use numbers effectively and to reason well.
3. *Spatial:* the ability to perceive the visual-spatial world accurately, and to perform transformations upon these perceptions.
4. *Bodily-Kinesthetic:* the ability to use one's whole body to express ideas and feelings, and facility in using one's hands to produce or transform things.
5. *Musical:* the capacity to perceive, discriminate, transform, and express musical forms.
6. *Interpersonal:* the ability to perceive and make distinctions in moods, intentions, motivations, and feelings of other people.
7. *Intrapersonal:* the capacity for self-knowledge and the ability to adapt oneself on the basis of that knowledge.
8. *Naturalist Intelligence:* the capacity for learning through the perception and generation of patterns (nature and the environment).

Some of the key points in Gardner's multiple intelligences theory are as follows:

- Every person possesses each of the intelligences.

- Most people can develop each intelligence to an adequate level of competency.
- Intelligences usually work together in complex ways.
- There are many ways to be intelligent within each category.

Gardner was quick to point out that this model of the different intelligences is a tentative one, and that after further research and investigation, additional intelligences may be identified as well.

Multiple intelligence (MI) theory, unlike other current learning style theories, is a cognitive model in that it seeks to describe how individuals use their intelligences to solve problems and create products. Unlike other models that are primarily process oriented, the MI approach is geared to how the human mind perceives and operates on the world's contents (such as objects and people). MI theory is more an attitude toward learning than a set program of fixed techniques and strategies. It provides educators with broad opportunities to creatively adapt its fundamental principles to any number of educational settings (see figures 3.1 and 3.2).

Developing a profile of a person's multiple intelligences is not a simple matter. There is no test to accurately determine the nature or quality of a person's intelligences. As Howard Gardner repeatedly points out, standardized tests measure only a small part of the total spectrum of abilities.

Multiple Intelligences Model

The theory of multiple intelligences is a good model for teachers to use when looking at their personal professional strengths and weaknesses, and also has broad implications for team teaching. In a school that is committed to developing students' multiple intelligences, the ideal teaching team would include members with expertise in all the intelligences, each member of the team possessing a high level of development in different intelligences. (For example, one teacher might have highly developed linguistic intelligence, while another excels in the logical-mathematical intelligence).

A key point in MI theory is that most people can develop all their intelligences to a relatively competent level of mastery. Whether or not these intelligences develop fully depends primarily on three factors:

- *Biological endowment:* this includes hereditary factors as well as insults or injuries to the brain before, during, and after birth.

continued on page 38

EIGHT WAYS OF TEACHING

INTELLIGENCE	TEACHING ACTIVITIES	TEACHING MATERIALS	INSTRUCTIONAL STRATEGIES
LINGUISTIC	lectures, discussions, word games, storytelling, choral, reading, journal writing	books, tapes, records, computers, stamp sets, books on tape	read about it, talk about it, listen to it
LOGICAL-MATHEMATICAL	critical thinking tasks, brain teasers, problem-solving math tasks, number games, mental calculations	calculators, computers, manipulatives, math games	think about it critically, conceptualize it, quantify it
SPATIAL	visual presentations, artistic activities, creative games, visualization	graphs, maps, videos, LEGO sets, art materials, optical illusions, cameras, picture library	see it, draw it, visualize it, color it, create it
BODILY-KINESTHETIC	hands-on learning, drama, dance, sports activities, tactile activities	building tools, clay, sports equipment, manipulatives, tactile learning resources	build it, act it out, touch it, "feel" it inside, dance it
MUSICAL	"rapping," lyrics and melodies that aid instruction	tapes and tape recorder, CDs and CD player, percussion, and other musical instruments	sing it, play it, "rap" it, listen to it
INTERPERSONAL	cooperative and collaborative learning, peer tutoring	board games, party supplies, props for role play	teach it to each other, collaborate on it, interact with it
INTRAPERSONAL	individualized instruction, independent study, alternative options in course of study	educational computer software, reflection guides, journals, materials for projects	connect it to your personal life, make choices in regard to it
NATURALIST	moving the learning environment outdoors	magnifying glass, guide books	connect it to nature, identify patterns, and connect previous experiences

Figure 3.1

EIGHT EDUCATIONAL APPROACHES AND TECHNIQUES

INTELLIGENCE	EDUCATIONAL MOVEMENT (PRIMARY INTELLIGENCE)	SAMPLE TEACHER PRESENTATION SKILL	SAMPLE ACTIVITY TO BEGIN A LESSON
LINGUISTIC	Whole Language	teach through storytelling	long word on chalkboard
LOGICAL-MATHEMATICAL	Critical Thinking	Socratic questioning	posing a logical paradox
SPATIAL	Integrated Arts Instruction	drawing/mind-mapping concepts	unusual illustrations on the overhead
BODILY-KINESTHETIC	Hands-on Learning	using gestures/dramatic expressions	mysterious artifact passed around classroom
MUSICAL	Suggestopedia: uses drama and visual aids as learning keys	using voice rhythmically	piece of music played as students come into class
INTERPERSONAL	Cooperative Learning	dynamically interacting with students	pair and share
INTRAPERSONAL	Individualized Instruction	bringing feeling into presentation	"Close your eyes and think of a time in your life when . . ."
NATURALIST	Experiential Learning	presenting information in context so that the learner can connect with previous experience	look for and identify patterns in nature

Figure 3.2

SkyLight Training and Publishing Inc.

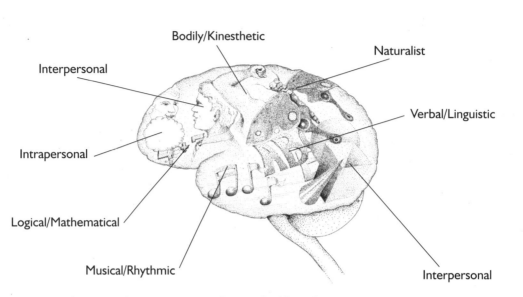

Interpersonal

Bodily/Kinesthetic

Naturalist

Intrapersonal

Verbal/Linguistic

Logical/Mathematical

Musical/Rhythmic

Interpersonal

From *Brain-Compatible Classrooms,* by Robin Fogarty. © 1997 by SkyLight Training and Publishing, Inc. Reprinted with permission of SkyLight Training and Publishing Inc., Arlington Heights, IL.

- *Personal life history:* this includes experiences with parents, teachers, peers, friends, and others who might influence intelligences in an either positive or negative manner.
- *Cultural and historical background:* this includes the time and place in which a person was born and raised.

MI theory is a model that values nurture as much as, and probably more than, nature in accounting for the development of intelligences. According to Gardner, there are two key junctures in the development of intelligences—experiences that represent turning points in the development of a person's talents and abilities. Critical positive experiences can provide the sparks that ignite an intelligence and start its progression and development, while traumatic or negative experiences can cause intelligences to "downshift" or completely "shut down." Such paralyzing or traumatic experiences are the ones that are often filled with shame, guilt, fear, anger, and other negative emotions that may inhibit or restrict the complete development of a budding intelligence.

MI theory offers a model of personal development that can help educators understand how their own personal learning style affects their classroom teaching style. It can be used to help the teacher become cognizant of his or her own shortcomings, and realize that each person has the power to activate those intelligences that have been underdeveloped or allowed to atrophy.

One of MI theory's greatest contributions to education is that it presents the case for teachers to expand the repertoire of techniques, tools, and strategies beyond the typical linguistic and logical ones which predominate in today's classrooms. It is not uncommon to find classroom teachers either talking at the students (lecturing) or spoon-feeding information to those students piecemeal. It is also probable that the students in these same classrooms will be doing written work which takes the form of workbooks or worksheets. Teaching with multiple intelligences in mind would mean instead using brain-compatible methodologies which involve the learner in the active discovery of knowledge, and provide a broad range of stimulating curricula to spark the varied intelligences to blaze to a higher developmental level.

Many contemporary alternative educational models essentially are multiple-intelligence systems that use different terminologies and place varying levels of emphasis upon the different intelligences. Cooperative learning, for example, places its greatest emphasis on interpersonal intelligence, yet a specific cooperative group activity such as the creation of a group display design for the teams' research data (spatial as well as bodily/kinesthetic) or the writing of a team song about mathematics (musical) can involve students in each of the other intelligences as well.

Simply put then, MI theory encompasses what good teachers have always done in their teaching: reach beyond the text and blackboard to spark student creativity, interest, and intelligence. MI theory provides a way for all teachers to reflect upon their best teaching methods, and to understand why these methods work. It also helps teachers expand their current teaching style to include a broader range of methods, thereby making use of the brain's inherent learning style to reach an even wider and more diverse range of learners.

> I believe that we should get away altogether from tests and correlations among tests, and look instead at more naturalistic sources of information about how people around the world develop skills important to their way of life. (Gardner 1987)

Assessment for Multiple Intelligences

Gardner's multiple intelligences theory requires that changes be made in assessment methods and techniques currently used to evaluate learning. It would be totally counterproductive to have students participate in various multispectrum experiences in all eight intelligences only to have them demonstrate their learning through narrowly focused standardized tests. Educators would be sending a double message to students as well as the community: (1) while learning through the use of eight intelligences is fun, novel, and exciting, (2) when it comes down to what is really important, knowledge must be tested the way it has always been tested—through norm-standardized tests that emphasize the memorization of isolated bits and pieces of information.

MI instruction requires a fundamental restructuring in the way educators assess student learning. Such instruction must be supported by a system that relies less on formal, standardized or norm-referenced tests, and more on authentic methods that are either criterion-referenced and benchmarked, or that compare students to their own past performances. It is Gardner's belief that authentic measures allow students to demonstrate what they've learned in context, in a setting that closely matches the environment in which they would be expected to use that learning in real life. Standardized instruments, on the other hand, almost always assess students in artificial settings, removed from any real-world context.

Performance-based learning projects, such as the ones in this book, provide the kind of educational restructuring that is compatible with the way the brain learns. The projects are authentic in that they grow out of real-life needs and experiences. The assessment is continuous and ongoing, allowing for numerous opportunities for feedback, revision, and adjustment in teaching strategy.

Perhaps the greatest contribution MI theory has made to assessment is the concept that there are multiple ways to evaluate student learning. The biggest shortcoming of standardized tests is that they require students to show in a narrowly defined way what they have learned during the school year. Standardized tests usually require that students be seated at a desk, that they complete the test within a specified time limit, and that they speak to no one during the test. The tests themselves usually contain largely linguistic questions or test items that students must answer by filling in bubbles on computerized test forms.

Assessment through the multiple intelligences, however, supports the belief that students should be able to show competence in a specific skill, subject, or content area in any number of ways. Just as the theory of multiple intelligences suggests that learning can be presented in at least eight different ways, it would follow that learning can be assessed in at least eight different ways. By linking learning to pictures, physical actions, musical phrases, sequential logical, social connections, nature, the environment, and personal feelings, students have increased opportunities to enlist their multiple intelligences in the articulation of their understanding. In other words, while many students may have mastered the material taught in school, they may not be able to successfully demonstrate this knowledge if the only setting available for competency demonstration is a narrowly focused linguistic testing arena.

Both the manner in which an assessment is presented and the method in which the student responds are crucial to the accuracy of the particular measuring tool used to determine that student's competence. If a student is a visual learner, yet is exposed only to the printed word when learning new material, then he or she probably will not be able to demonstrate mastery of the subject. The kinds of assessment experiences that MI theory supports (especially those that are project-based and thematically oriented) offer students frequent opportunities to be exposed to multiple contexts in any given period.

As students increasingly engage in multiple-intelligence projects and activities, the opportunities for documenting their learning in portfolio-type assessments expands considerably. In the past decade, portfolio development has often been limited to work requiring the linguistic and logical/mathematical intelligences (writing portfolios and math portfolios). Both MI theory and brain research, however, seem to suggest that portfolios ought to be expanded to include materials from all the different intelligences. Such portfolios might include project work, photos, diagrams, videotapes, audiotapes, written feedback from teachers and peers, self-assessment essays, etc.

Since MI assessment and MI instruction represent flip sides of the same coin, these approaches to assessment would not take more time to implement. The assessments are integral to the instruction, and as such, the assessment experiences and instructional experiences become indistinguishable. Students engaged in this process come to regard the assessment experience as just another opportunity to learn.

The educational paradigm shift towards brain-based learning and cognitive psychology has educators increasingly interested in helping students learn and develop thinking strategies.

How students think has become as important as what they think about. Research studies such as the Third International Mathematics and Science Study (TIMSS) demonstrate that while over the past few years American students have been able to improve their performance on rote learning tasks such as spelling and arithmetic, their ability to use higher thinking skills and do problem-solving tasks ranks low when compared to students in other countries. Consequently, more and more educators are looking for ways to help students think more effectively when confronted with academic problems.

Over forty years ago, University of Chicago professor Benjamin S. Bloom (1956) unveiled his famous "taxonomy of educational objectives." Bloom's six levels of cognitive complexity have been used over the past four decades as a gauge by which educators can ensure that instruction stimulates and develops students' higher order thinking abilities.

The six taxonomy levels are:

- *Knowledge:* rote memory skills such as poem memorization (linguistic intelligence) or memorization of a piece of music (musical intelligence).
- *Comprehension:* the ability to translate, paraphrase, and interpret written or spoken language (linguistic intelligence), or the extrapolation of material as in the solving of algebra and/or geometry problems (logical/mathematical intelligence).
- *Application:* the capacity to transfer knowledge from one setting to another, as in sports, where what is learned in practice is applied during a game or competition situation (bodily/kinesthetic intelligence).
- *Analysis:* the breaking down of concepts into their constituent parts as when learning a new song or dance routine (musical intelligence or bodily/kinesthetic intelligence).
- *Synthesis:* the combining of constituent elements into an entity or making connections as with the design of geometry proofs (logical/mathematical intelligence).
- *Evaluation:* the process whereby standards are set to judge the quality of the component parts as in self-reflective journal writings (intrapersonal intelligence).

Bloom's taxonomy provides a quality-control mechanism through which educators can evaluate how deeply students' minds have been stirred by a multiple-intelligence curriculum. MI curriculum can be designed to incorporate all of Bloom's levels of cognitive complexity. MI theory represents a model that enables educators to move beyond heavily linguistic lower order thinking activities (for example, worksheets) into a broader range of complex cognitive tasks that make better use of the brain's natural affinities and prepares students to function in the adult world of jobs and responsibilities. (See figure 3.3 for a chart of assessment vocabulary words compatible with Bloom's ideas.)

Howard Gardner's theory of multiple intelligences has provided the educational community with a language that speaks to the strengths and inner gifts of all children, not only those who happen to learn in either the linguistic or logical-mathematical mode. The multiple intelligences call for a new curriculum design, one capable of communicating with the unique brain of each learner, speaking that individual's language, and best met in a classroom environment conducive to cooperative learning (see figure 3.4).

ASSESSMENT VOCABULARY BASED ON "BLOOM'S TAXONOMY" OF COGNITIVE FUNCTION

COGNITIVE DOMAIN	DESCRIPTIVE VERBS	ASSESSMENT WORDS & PHRASES
KNOWLEDGE	explain, identify, define, list, describe, name, classify	describe . . . select . . . who, what, where, when, why, how, which one, how much
COMPREHENSION	explain, outline, propose, infer, modify, vary, summarize, change	what does this mean? rephrase or restate in your own words . . . explain why . . . summarize, outline . . .
APPLICATION	explain, estimate, plan, solve, predict	explain what would happen if . . . what and how much would change if . . .?
ANALYSIS	identify, compare, contrast, equate, examine, deduce	what conclusions can be made from . . .? what is the relationship of . . .? which concepts are the most important?
SYNTHESIS	create, design, plan, imagine, set up	create, design, choose, plan
EVALUATION	evaluate, judge, assess, determine, conclude, critique, rank	which is more valid/ logical/appropriate? compare and contrast critique . . .

Figure 3.3

SkyLight Training and Publishing Inc.

NEW BRAIN RESEARCH AND TWELVE IMPLICATIONS FOR TEACHING

Caine and Caine 1997

Recent Research Suggests	Teaching Suggestions
1. The brain performs many functions simultaneously. Learning is enhanced by a rich environment containing a variety of stimuli.	1. Present content through a variety of teaching strategies, such as physical activities, individualized learning times, group interactions, artistic variations, and musical interpretations to help orchestrate student experiences.
2. Learning engages the entire physiology. Physical development, personal comfort, and emotional state affect the ability to learn.	2. Be aware that children mature at different rates; chronological age may not reflect the student's readiness to learn. Incorporate facets of health (stress management, nutrition, and exercise) into the learning process.
3. The search for meaning is innate. The mind's natural curiosity can be engaged by complex and meaningful challenges.	3. Seek to present lessons and activities that stimulate the mind's natural curiosity and affinity for meaning.
4. The brain is designed to perceive and generate patterns.	4. Present information in context (e.g., real-life science and mathematics, thematic instruction) so the learner can identify patterns and connect with previous experiences.

Figure 3.4

Recent Research Suggests	Teaching Suggestions
5. Emotions and cognition cannot be separated. Emotions can be crucial to the storage and recall of information.	5. Help build a classroom environment that promotes positive attitudes among students and teachers and about class work. Encourage students to be aware of their feelings and how the emotional climate affects their learning.
6. Every brain simultaneously perceives and creates parts and wholes.	6. Try to avoid isolating information from its context. Such isolation makes learning more difficult. Design activities that require full brain interaction and communication.
7. Learning involves both focused attention and peripheral perception.	7. Be aware that the teacher's enthusiasm, modeling, and coaching present important signals about the value of what is being learned.
8. Learning always involves conscious and unconscious processes.	8. Use "hooks" or other motivational techniques to encourage personal connections. Encourage "active processing" through reflection and metacognition to help students consciously review their learning.

SkyLight Training and Publishing Inc.

Recent Research Suggests	Teaching Suggestions
9. We have at least two types of memory: spatial, which registers our daily experience; and rote learning, which deals with facts and skills in isolation.	9. Separating information and skills from prior experience forces the learner to depend on rote memory. Try to avoid an emphasis on rote learning; it ignores the learner's personal side and interferes with subsequent development of understanding.
10. The brain understands best when facts and skills are embedded in natural spatial memory.	10. Use techniques that create or reflect real world experiences and use varied senses. Examples include demonstrations, projects, and integration of content areas that embed ideas in genuine experience.
11. Learning is enhanced by challenge and inhibited by threat.	11. Try to create an atmosphere of "relaxed alertness" that is low in threat and high in challenge (a safe place for experimenting and taking chances).
12. Each brain is unique. The brain's structure is actually changed by learning.	12. Use multifaceted teaching strategies to attract individual interests and let students express their auditory, visual, tactile, or emotional preferences.

CHAPTER 4

PERFORMANCE-BASED INSTRUCTIONAL STRATEGIES

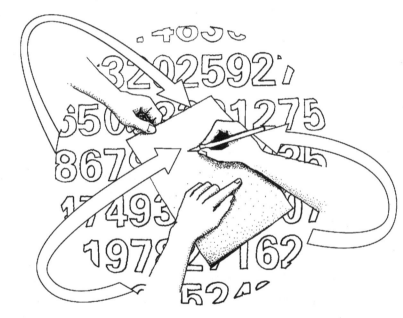

Human beings have been successful as a species; unlike tigers, big elephants, lizards, or gazelles who fend for themselves, we as humans are intelligent. But an intelligent man or woman in the jungle or forest would not survive alone. What has really made the human such a successful species is our ability to apply our intelligence to cooperation with others in order to accomplish group goals. Therefore, our society is composed of cooperative groups—(families, neighborhoods, work groups, political parties, clubs and teams). These groups also have a competitive element, but in all of them, if the individual cannot cooperate to achieve a common goal, all lose.

—Slavin 1981

Cooperative/collaborative instruction employing performance assessment offers a learning methodology that students find comfortable since these techniques provide a way to learn and process new information in a brain-compatible manner. Much of the recent brain research provides powerful biological justification for the shift away from traditional methodologies of instruction, learning, and assessment. Assessment strategies that are brain-compatible have the following common characteristics:

- They conform to current theories on how the brain learns.
- They promote psychological safety, risk taking, and experimentation.
- They view assessment as a process for continuous improvement.
- They use a full range of multiple intelligences.

Recent brain research demonstrates that intelligence can be altered through the creation of new neural pathways in the brain. Children in particular have certain windows of opportunity during which specific skills such as language skills are more easily learned. Because of the existence of these windows, the first few years of a child's life are critically important to his or her future.

This knowledge is both a burden as well as an opportunity for the educator. It is a burden, since with this knowledge we are morally and ethically obligated to provide every child with an opportunity to reach his or her full development potential; it is also an opportunity, since we have proof that a child's intelligence can be altered. Educators need to focus on not only a child's early years but on his or her adolescence as well. If, in fact, these windows of opportunity are not closed off, people can retain the capacity to grow intellectually throughout their lives. This is the potential that must be cultivated if individuals are to become life-long learners.

In order to do this innovative work, we need to provide children with a very different kind of education from that which is currently in place. Having children sit in one place for extended periods of time without any pause for reflection or discussion does not lead to self-directed, metacognitve development. Everyone needs some downtime for processing. Much of our learning takes place through the processes of introspection, reflection, dialogue, and discussion which then fosters greater retention of information and a deeper and more complex understanding for application.

Cooperative Learning

The premise that forms the basis for cooperative learning is that if individuals cannot develop the capacity to work together for the achievement of a greater purpose, they all will lose in the end. It is vital that teachers develop a sense of how and when to structure students' learning goals competitively, individualistically, or cooperatively. While each of these structures has its place, in an ideal learning environment all three goal structures would be used simultaneously. Students would compete for fun as in math team meets or math relay games. They would work autonomously as when writing a proof in defense of a geometry hypothesis, practicing a skill that needs improvement, or when writing reflective journal entries. And they would learn to collaborate with each other on team projects or team experiences as when preparing a bid to be submitted for a house-painting job.

Often, *competitive* classroom situations are not beneficial for all students because in this type of situation the students must compete with one another to achieve a goal that only one or very few students can attain. For example, the administration of a qualifying round of tests usually creates a highly stressful situation for students, since in this kind of testing situation students are usually graded on a curve. This pushes the students to work as quickly and accurately as they can in opposition to their peers because the perception is that they can only obtain their individual goals at the expense of others in their class. This results in a negative interdependence among goal achievements, since in this learning dynamic the students are trying to secure an outcome beneficial to them, yet detrimental to their classmates.

In the *individually* structured environment, students work by themselves to accomplish learning goals unrelated to the performance of others. An example of this would be a student writing a geometry proof to defend a particular hypothesis. Goals are assigned, and student efforts are evaluated against a fixed set of standards with rewards granted accordingly. Students work at their own pace, independent of the other students in the class. In such individualistic learning activities, students understand that their achievements are not related to what the other students do. In this situation, students try to achieve a result that is personally beneficial and will see the goal achievements of others as irrelevant.

In the *cooperatively* structured classroom, students find that they must work together in order to accomplish their mutual goal. Individuals in small groups are assigned information and/or materials for which all the group members are responsible. In a cooperative learning environment this produces a positive interdependence among the students. The students' perception is that the learning goals can be reached only if all the group members are successful. The students therefore seek outcomes that are beneficial to all those with whom they are working. In order to achieve this result, they need to discuss the information and/or material with each other, help one another understand it, and encourage each other to work hard. An example of this is the survey project in chapter 9 of this book (see Lesson 3: Which Graph Works Best?). In this project, all students must understand how the survey is to be conducted, what is needed for the construction of accurate high-quality graph displays, and what will be said during their presentation before the class.

Each of these three learning environments is beneficial when used constructively:

- The *competitive* environment is beneficial in keeping students "on their toes" (*competitive* in this case should be construed as a minimum level of stress and a maximum level of challenge).
- The *individual* learning environment is beneficial in helping develop those introspective and self-evaluative skills necessary for metacognitive growth as well as for practice and rehearsal of possible problem areas.
- The *cooperative* learning environment is beneficial in that students must learn to work together in order to accomplish mutual goals.

Classroom activities should provide students the opportunity to work both individually and in small and large group arrangements. . . . Working in small groups provides students with opportunities to talk about ideas and listen to their peers, enables teachers to interact more closely with students, takes positive advantage of the social characteristics of the middle student, and provides opportunities for students to exchange ideas and hence develop their ability to communicate and reason. (NCTM 1989)

It is the teacher's responsibility to develop an effective environment and an effective pedagogy, both conducive to cooperative learning. Such an environment can be created by forming competent student groups, using lessons that require team problem solving, and developing methods to monitor both group work and individual learning. (See figures 4.1, 4.2, and 4.3 for some tools to help facilitate group activities.)

Unfortunately, many teachers who believe they are using cooperative learning are in fact missing its essence. There is a critical difference between simply putting students into groups to learn and in structuring cooperative interdependence among students. Having students side-by-side at the same table to talk with each other as they do their individual assignments is not cooperative learning, although such an activity does have a place in the classroom. Cooperative learning is not assigning a report to a group of students and having one student do the work while the others put in nothing more than their names on the end product. Cooperative learning is the instructional use of small groups where students maximize their own and each other's learning synergistically.

In cooperative learning situations, students look to their peers rather than the teacher for assistance, feedback, reinforcement, and support. They share materials, interact, and encourage each other. They explain the necessary information to one another, and elaborate on the strategies and concepts they need to use. These exchanges between group members and the intellectual challenges that result from conflicting ideas and conclusions are what promote critical thinking, higher level reasoning, and metacognitive thought—the knowledge of one's own thinking processes and strategies, as well as the ability to consciously reflect and act on the knowledge of cognition in order to modify those processes and strategies. It's the act of explaining what one knows to other group members and the development of essential listening skills that together foster the understanding of how to apply knowledge and skills to new and different situations.

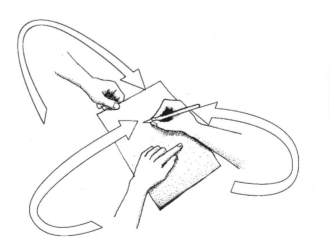

To support individual student accountability, it is beneficial to assign specific roles to each of the group

continued on page 57

DESCRIPTION OF COOPERATIVE GROUP ACTIVITY ROLES

The following is part of the class introductory lesson on roles and behaviors for cooperative group learning.

Students are to be divided into groups of three or four, every member of the group having a specific job and tasks to perform. When there are groups of three individuals, the roles of resource manager and materials manager may be combined.

ROLE ASSIGNMENTS

Coordinator
- Takes part in and contributes to the group activity
- Gets the group settled down and started on the activity
- Directs the activity and keeps all group members on task
- Encourages all members to contribute to discussions
- Helps group members to agree on answers to questions
- Reminds members to keep voices low during discussions

Recorder
- Takes part in and contributes to the group activity
- Keeps notes on all activities for group log entries (see figure 4.2)
- Prepares a copy of the activity log sheet (see figure 4.3) to be turned in to the teacher at the end of the class

Materials Manager
- Takes part in and contributes to the group activity
- Picks up and distributes activity log sheets
- Picks up and distributes manipulatives and/or project supplies in an efficient manner
- Assumes responsibility for the care of manipulatives and/or project supplies
- Collects and turns in manipulatives and/or project supplies

Resource Manager
- Takes part in and contributes to the group activity
- Finds additional resource materials when needed
- Decides when help is needed, and then asks the teacher for that help

Figure 4.1

SkyLight Training and Publishing Inc.

COOPERATIVE GROUP ACTIVITY NOTES

Date: _____

NAMES OF GROUP MEMBERS

_____

_____

_____

ROLE ASSIGNMENTS

Coordinator: _____

Recorder: _____

Materials Manager: _____

Resource Manager: _____

PROJECT ASSIGNMENT

_____

_____

_____

_____

_____

_____

Due Date: _____

NOTES FOR TODAY'S CLASS

_____

_____

_____

_____

_____

_____

_____

_____

_____

_____

_____

Figure 4.2

COOPERATIVE GROUP ACTIVITY LOG

Group Members:

_____

_____

Math Section: _____ Group Name: _____

Project:

_____
_____
_____
_____
_____

Date	Name	Work Completed

Figure 4.3

SkyLight Training and Publishing Inc.

members. As the students begin interacting as teams, the members learn how their roles can complement and interconnect with their task. These roles can later be rotated to help create a positive interdependence and teach students new and different skills. With experience, students will learn to shift from role to role.

According to Johnson, Johnson, and Holubec (1988), successful implementation of cooperative learning requires that five basic elements be in place. The first element, that of *positive interdependence,* refers to the concept that the students will either "sink or swim together." To achieve this end, the students' mutual goals must first be established (goal interdependence). There must also be division of labor (task interdependence); division of materials, resources, or information among group members (resource interdependence); and the assignment of specific jobs or roles to each group member (role interdependence).

Positive educational outcomes are the result of the second element, *face-to-face interaction.* This refers to the positive interaction patterns and verbal exchanges that take place among students in carefully structured cooperative groups. Verbal summaries, giving and receiving explanations, and elaborations (relating the new learning to previous learning) are all varieties of verbal exchanges.

Individual accountability is the third element. Cooperative learning groups will not succeed unless every member has learned the information and/or material, or has helped with and understands the assignment. For this reason it is essential that the teacher frequently promote and assess individual progress (proactive and preemptive guidance) so that team members can support and help each other.

The fourth element is *interpersonal and small group skills.* Students rarely come to school with the social skills necessary for effective collaboration. It is up to the teacher to instruct them in appropriate communication, leadership, trust, decision-making, and conflict-management skills as well as provide the motivation to use such skills to ensure effective group dynamics. Children are not born instinctively knowing how to cooperate with others. Learning how to interact with others is just like learning other basic skills. (See figure 4.4 for some class exercises that might help the students to internalize such processing.)

T-CHART CONSTRUCTION

Constructing a T-chart may be useful if the necessary social skills are lacking from the group or an individual. To construct a T-chart:

1. Write the name of the skill to be learned and practiced and draw a large *T* underneath.

2. Title the left side of the *T* "Looks Like" and the right side of the *T* "Sounds Like."

3. On the left side write a number of behaviors that demonstrate or reinforce the skill concept. On the right side write a number of phrases that display the concept.

APPROVAL

Looks Like	Sounds Like
Nodding head	"Good idea!"
Thumbs up	"I like that!"
Smiling while listening	"Way to go!"

4. Have the students practice "looks like" and "sounds like" several times before beginning the lesson.

Figure 4.4

Other suggestions for promoting the cooperative and collaborative skills associated with positive group relationships include the following:

- praising good ideas
- describing feelings
- expressing support for one another
- listening to each other
- being positive
- giving encouragement

For small group work to be successful, the team members must learn to function as a unit. The best way to achieve such behavior is for the teacher to make the expectation absolutely clear that when solving a problem, all students must be able to explain their thinking, to justify their answers, and to explain why an answer is reasonable. When students defend their solutions to others in small groups, they develop a better understanding of the mathematics involved, and become more confident about their own ability to solve difficult problems.

The following three components are needed for the establishment of an environment conducive to small group problem-solving work:

1. Students are expected to work together on their assigned problem and make sure that each member of the group participates.
2. Students are expected to listen to each other carefully, and to then build on each other's ideas.
3. Each individual team member is expected to be able to explain and justify the team solution.

For students to understand mathematics conceptually, they need to interact with each other as well as the teacher, and discuss their own ideas about mathematics.

The following cooperative skills starters use temporary, informal groups that last from a few minutes to one class period. They are often utilized so that students can engage in focused discussion before and after a lesson. The following ideas were derived from the work of Johnson, Johnson, and Holubec (1988).

1. *Target Groups:* Before beginning a video, lesson, or reading assignment, students should identify what they already know about the

subject and identify questions they may have about it. Afterwards, the groups can answer questions, discuss new information, and formulate new questions.

2. *Neighbor to Neighbor:* Have the students ask their neighbor something about the lesson: to explain a new concept, to summarize the most important points of the discussion, or to do something else that might fit the lesson.

3. *Study-Buddies:* Students compare their homework answers, discuss any problems they haven't answered similarly, go over those problems together, and then list the reasons they changed any of the answers. They then make sure that all their answers match. The teacher needs to grade only one randomly selected paper from each group, and then gives all group members that same grade (since all their answers should match).

4. *Problem Detectives:* Groups are given a problem to solve. Each student must contribute to part of the solution. Groups can decide who does what, but they must show how each member contributed. An alternative strategy is for the group to decide on the solution together, but then each group member must be able to independently explain how the problem was solved.

5. *Drill Pairs:* Students drill each other on the facts they need to know until they are certain both partners know and can remember them all. This works for math, spelling, vocabulary, grammar, test review, etc.

The fifth and final basic element for the successful implementation of cooperative learning is *group processing.* Processing refers to giving students the time and the procedural skills necessary to analyze how well their groups are functioning and whether or not they are making use of the required social skills. Processing provides accurate, non-threatening feedback on the procedures the group is using to achieve its goals. The feedback gives group members information that helps them improve their performance.

Cooperative learning is not a new idea. The most successful individuals are those who are able to organize and coordinate efforts for a common purpose. However, simply placing students in groups and instructing them to work together will not in and of itself achieve this desired goal of collaboration. Deliberate and planned instruction in socialization skills is usually necessary for cooperation among group members to occur. The formula for success most often is a teacher with good classroom management skills and a well-structured classroom environment. Such an environment might appear to an outsider as disorganized, but in reality it is a form of "organized chaos." The children are all moving about the room discussing their project work, working on different project aspects simultaneously, and contributing to a certain level of noise. In actuality, however, each of them is on task and working toward their common purpose.

Writing in the Classroom

> The development of a student's power to use mathematics involves learning the signs, symbols, and terms of mathematics. This is best accomplished in problem situations in which students have an opportunity to read, write, and discuss ideas in which the use of the language of mathematics becomes natural. As students communicate their ideas, they learn to clarify, refine, and consolidate their thinking. (NCTM 1989)

Along with the disappointment in traditional education and the call for higher standards, come new theories of learning, and mathematics is no exception. The 1989 NCTM "Standards" document is very specific in its emphasis of the means by which middle school students are to increase their levels of "mathematical literacy":

> Implementation of the 5-8 standards [middle-level] should consider the unique characteristics of the middle school student . . . throughout this period. . . . Concrete experience should continue to provide the means by which they construct knowledge. From these experiences they abstract more complex meanings and ideas. The use of language, both written and oral, helps students clarify their thinking and report their observations as they form and verify their mathematical ideas. (NCTM 1989)

The original Standards document specifies communication as an area where a shift in emphasis is needed. It specifically names discussion, writing, reading, and hearing about mathematical ideas as those areas in need of increased attention. It lists as areas for decreased emphasis the activities of doing fill-in-the-blank worksheets and answering questions requiring responses such as only yes, no, or a number.

Students have a better chance of success with such discussion, writing, reading, and hearing about mathematical ideas if there is group discussion and individual verbalization before beginning problem elaborations or reflections.

Below are some sample questions teachers can use to help guide students in some of the written aspects of their reflections.

1. *Understanding of the Problem*
   - Can you tell me in your own words what this problem is about?
   - Is anything missing, or has any unnecessary information been given?
   - What assumptions are you making about the problem?

2. *Planning of the Strategy*
   - Can you explain your strategy to me?
   - What have you tried so far?
   - How did you organize your information?
   - Is there a simpler problem related to this one that you could solve first?

3. *Executing the Strategy*
   - Can you show me how you checked your work?
   - Why did you organize your work in this way?
   - Why did you draw this diagram?
   - How do you know whether what you are doing is correct?

4. *Review of the Work*
   - Are you sure your answer is correct? How do you know this?
   - Could you have solved this problem differently?
   - What made you decide to use this strategy?
   - If I changed the original problem to read . . ., would you still use this same strategy?

5. *Mathematical Communication*
   - Can you reword this problem using simpler terms?
   - Can you explain why you are doing this?
   - How would you explain what you are doing to a teammate who is confused?
   - Can you create a problem of your own using this same strategy?

6. *Mathematical Connections*
   - Have you ever solved a problem similar to this one? In what way is it the same? In what ways is it different? [Show the student a different but similar problem, then ask:] What, if anything, is similar about the mathematics in this problem and the one you just solved?

7. *Self-Assessment*
   - Is this kind of problem easy or hard for you?
   - What makes this type of problem easy? What makes it difficult?
   - In general, what kinds of problems are especially hard for you? What kinds are easy? Why?

Metacognitive self-reflections are an effective means of assessing feelings and beliefs about mathematics as well as other information. In a self-reflection, students are often asked to write a retrospective account of the work completed. They reflect on the experience, describe their methods and results, and assess what new information they have learned. The teacher can lend some structure to the reflection by asking students to respond to questions that focus on selected aspects of the activity, for example:
- Describe the task you did for your group.
- How did you keep track of your results?
- How confident do you (or don't you) feel about the work you did? Why?
- What new mathematics did you learn?
- How does this new knowledge relate to knowledge you already have?
- What new questions do you now have after completing this activity?

In its *1997–98 Handbook: NCTM Goals, Leaders, and Position Statements,* the National Council of Teachers of Mathematics states, "Teachers should not rely on paper-and-pencil tests and timed drills as their only means to judge students' performance" (1997). The Council's position is that such tests are and always will be needed; however, these tests should not be the only method used: "Students should be given ample opportunity to demonstrate their mathematical understanding through a variety of methods including portfolios, discussions, presentations, and projects in addition to the traditional approach of written tests. This variety enables teachers to review, assess, and gauge students' progress" (1997).

Classroom Practice

While assessment should be the central aspect of classroom practice linking curriculum, teaching, and learning, it is primarily being used today at the end of instructional units to both assign grades and differentiate the successful students from the unsuccessful. Traditional assessment methods such as paper-and-pencil chapter tests have always relied heavily on the completion and evaluation of imitative exercises and routine problems.

The NCTM Standards present a vision of assessment that is highly compatible with MI and brain-based learning in that it is ongoing and carried out in multiple and varied ways. By using the eight intelligences as a guide for instruction and evaluation; by listening to, observing, and talking with students; by asking students questions to help reveal their reasoning; by examining students' individual or group written and/or project work, teachers are able to develop an accurate and valid picture of what students know and can do. When conceived of and used in a constructive manner, MI and brain-based assessments provide the means of gaining true insight into students' thinking and reasoning abilities. In addition, assessment can be a powerful tool to help teachers monitor the effectiveness of their own teaching, judge the utility of the learning tasks, and consider when and where to go next in instruction.

Because cooperative learning as an instructional methodology is so highly socialized, it is also extremely brain-compatible. Socialization is important to the learning process, and a great deal of socialization comes into play in a cooperative learning classroom environment. Recent brain research has shown how the human brain is a social brain and therefore needs a social context for optimum learning to occur. Socialization and communication are also conducive to brainstorming sessions. Such sessions are employed when students engage in the development of problem-solving strategies. While problem-solving strategies and critical thinking skills are necessary for group tasks, instruction in such vital skills has often been neglected. Chapter 5 deals directly with problem-solving strategy instruction.

CHAPTER 5

PROBLEM-SOLVING STRATEGIES

"Few students spontaneously generate and use strategies on their own... [educators] need to explicitly teach these thinking and learning strategies."

—McTighe 1996

The human brain is a social brain needing a social context for optimum learning. Socialization and communication are also needed for fruitful brainstorming sessions. Such sessions are vital to the development of effective problem-solving strategies. While problem-solving strategies and critical thinking skills are needed for successful collaborative and individual work, instruction in these vital skills has often been neglected. This chapter deals directly with the instruction of six different problem-solving strategies:

- problem-solving heuristics (instructive methods that aid learning through exploration),
- study skills,
- thinking skills,
- thinking processes,
- mnemonic techniques (which serve as a cueing structure to facilitate recall, for example, acronyms, rhyming, sequence linking), and
- organizational strategies.

Competencies must be taught clearly and explicitly if the goal of performance improvement is to be reached. Strategies such as problem-solving heuristics, self-moderating strategies, thinking skills processes, mnemonic techniques, study skills, and organizational strategies are all highly teachable, and translate directly into improved performance results. Good direct instruction includes information about not only what a particular technique is, but how and when to use it (see figure 5.1 for some activities to help students learn these strategies). Following is an effective technique for solving multi-step problems:

1. Examine the problem.
2. Determine what information is given and what information can be implied.
3. Break the problem down into smaller units so that it becomes more manageable. (Try to find smaller, simpler shapes within the large, complex one.)
4. Plan a strategy—a step-by-step plan as to how you will solve the problem. Write out the strategy so that you can check to see if you have completed all the steps at the end.
5. Write out all the formulas you will need for this problem.
6. Solve the problem.
7. Check the strategy plan to be sure that you have done all the necessary steps, and labeled all answers correctly.

ACTIVITIES FOR LEARNING PROBLEM-SOLVING STRATEGIES

1. Brainstorm.

2. Make it simpler.

3. Use logical reasoning.

4. Work backwards.

5. Make a picture or diagram.

6. Make a chart or a table.

7. Make an organized list.

8. Use or look for a pattern.

9. Guess and check.

Figure 5.1

68

Problem-Solving Heuristics

Heuristics are instructive methods that aid learning through exploration and experimentation, especially trial and error. George Polya, in his book *How to Solve It: A New Aspect of Mathematical Method,* offers an assortment of methods and techniques for problem-solving in mathematics. An example of a problem-solving heuristic is a strategies wheel (see figures 5.2 and 5.3). Strategy wheels help students choose from among the different methodologies in their repertoire when trying to assess their best solution path. The first wheel (figure 5.2) has fewer choices and is more appropriate for students in earlier grades. More advanced students can have the choice of a greater number of methodologies since these will be used at more sophisticated levels (figure 5.3). The different sections represent the different choices that can be used individually or in any combination to arrive at the solution goal. An arrow pointing to the solution in use keeps the student focused on the particular methodology being used at that moment.

Individual students as well as student teams can refer to strategy wheels while solving problems. This helps remind them of various strategies taught in class and also helps them stay focused on the task at hand.

Problem-Solving Strategies Wheel

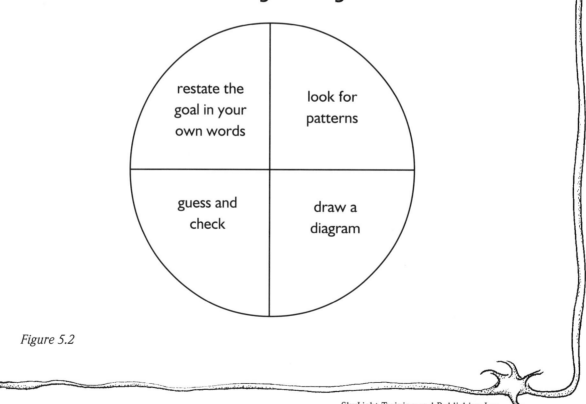

Figure 5.2

Advanced Strategies Wheel

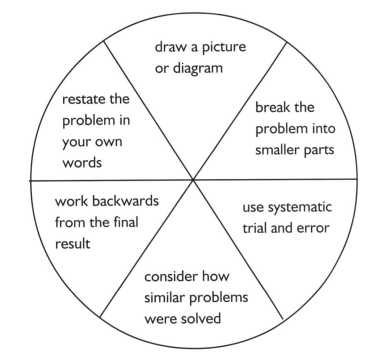

Figure 5.3

Study Skills, Thinking Skills, and Thinking Processes

Reading to perform a task is an example of a *study skill* needed for solving mathematics problems such as word or story problems. Following is a checklist for reading success. As they read, have your students remember to do these steps:

- Read all directions once to get a general idea of the problem or task.
- Read the material again to learn the specific directions.
- Summarize each direction on paper in your own words.
- Pay close attention to the pictures or diagrams provided.
- Pause after each direction you read, and make a picture in your mind of what you are supposed to do.
- When you come to something important that you don't understand, reread it or ask someone for help.

- Use resources such as your textbook glossary or a dictionary to look up any words you don't understand.
- Try to think ahead to anticipate any difficulty you might have.

Thinking skills, sometimes referred to as skills of cognitive learning, indicate the mental skills and processes involved in the act of learning, such as remembering and understanding facts or ideas. In recent years cognitive psychologists have compiled a great deal of new information about thinking and learning, much of it done in conjunction with neurobiologists interested in how the human brain learns to think, learn, and remember.

Cognitive processes, or *thinking processes,* are concerned with describing what goes on in the learner's brain during learning, that is, how knowledge is acquired, organized, stored in memory, and used in further learning and problem solving. It is often helpful to classify knowledge as either declarative (knowledge about something) or procedural (knowledge of how to do something). Some theorists suggest that knowledge begins as declarative, but becomes procedural as it is used in solving problems. The prior knowledge and experience that students bring to new learning situations critically affect how they learn and build new knowledge.

Mnemonic Techniques

Mnemonic techniques, devices employed to assist students in learning new information, can help to a limited degree, since mnemonics help to cue recall and connections to previously learned material. The technique, however, does not promote comprehension of underlying mathematical concepts, and is therefore extremely limited in its effectiveness.

Working memory, the number of things an individual can remember at a given time, is limited. For a small child, it may be only one item; for an adult, the limit is around seven items. Once that limit has been reached, no new information can enter the working memory without pushing something else out. To compensate, we must develop increasingly sophisticated thinking and learning strategies. This involves the grouping of items so that they only take up a single space of working memory, and the automatization of lower-level procedures into higher ones so that task execution becomes unconscious and automatic.

Learners remember new information best when it can be related to and incorporated with existing material already learned. Use of a mnemonic aid provides a cueing structure to trigger recall. These structures take the form of words in sentences or rhymes, or of visual images.

Rhyme technique refers to a technique that employs a familiar rhyme scheme to aid memory. A memory model designed by O'Keefe and Nadel (1978) suggests that our brain has a set of systems for receiving relatively unrelated information. One system, motivated by reward and punishment, makes up that part of our brain geared to rote memorization. There is also a spatial/autobiographical memory that does not need rehearsal, and which allows for instant recall of experiences (usually motivated by novelty). Meaningful learning occurs through a combination of these two.

Rhyme helps to cue those synapses involved in rote memory, making this technique useful for remembering things that cannot be learned in any other way, such as memorization of the multiplication tables. An example of a rhyme technique used to help students learn fraction division is "Yours is not to question why. Just invert and multiply." This rhyme can help students to remember the algorithm for the unit test, but its use is limited. It does not promote the comprehension of the underlying concepts involved in fraction division, nor does it increase mathematical understanding. It may be effective as a cueing device, but I do not recommend any cueing device as a basis for instruction.

Acronym techniques involve creating a new word from the first letters of a series of words to be learned. For example, the name of the Indian chief SOH-CAH-TOA is sometimes used to help students recall trigonometric functions.

$$\textbf{S}ine = \frac{\textbf{O}pposite\ side}{\textbf{H}ypotenuse} \qquad \textbf{C}osine = \frac{\textbf{A}djacent\ side}{\textbf{H}ypotenuse}$$

$$\textbf{T}angent = \frac{\textbf{O}pposite\ side}{\textbf{A}djacent\ side}$$

Retention and recall can improve when the teacher provides students with a mnemonic aid. While mnemonic devices do not help the learner comprehend and integrate new material into previous learning, they do serve to enhance recall. Reliance on the mnemonic aid decreases with repeated usage to trigger a particular information set. When and under what circumstances to provide mnemonic devices is a judgment call individual teachers will have to make.

Organizational Strategies

Teaching aids such as graphic organizers, graphic representations, drawings, and diagrams are all examples of organizational strategies.

Graphic organizers provide a visual, holistic representation of facts, concepts, and their relationship within an organized framework. They are effective tools that support thinking and learning by helping students and teachers to represent abstract information in a more concrete format, depict relationships between and among facts and concepts, relate new information to prior knowledge, and organize thoughts for writing or problem solving.

Teachers who include graphic organizers as part of their instructional repertoire enhance student learning, because knowledge that has been organized into a holistic conceptual framework is more easily remembered and understood than unstructured, unconnected bits of information. ("Holistic" here refers to the conceptual framework as a single entity rather than the sum of the parts it comprises.)

Graphic organizers exist in a variety of forms such as the concept web, flowchart, matrix, concept map, or Venn diagram (see figure 5.4). This last organizer can be used for a number of purposes, such as comparing.

Also, graphic organizers can be used prior to instructional activities as a conceptual framework for the integration of new information. During instruction they help students actively process and reorganize information. Following instruction they help students summarize learning and encourage elaboration, provide students with a structure for review, and help the teacher assess the level of student understanding.

Graphic representation strategies are learning tools that create symbolic pictures of the structure and relationship of the material. Some examples of graphic representation strategies are networking strategies that require students to depict relationships among concepts or ideas using a diagram format, and concept mapping strategies that require students to identify elements of the problem and then note them in proper sequence.

Venn Diagram

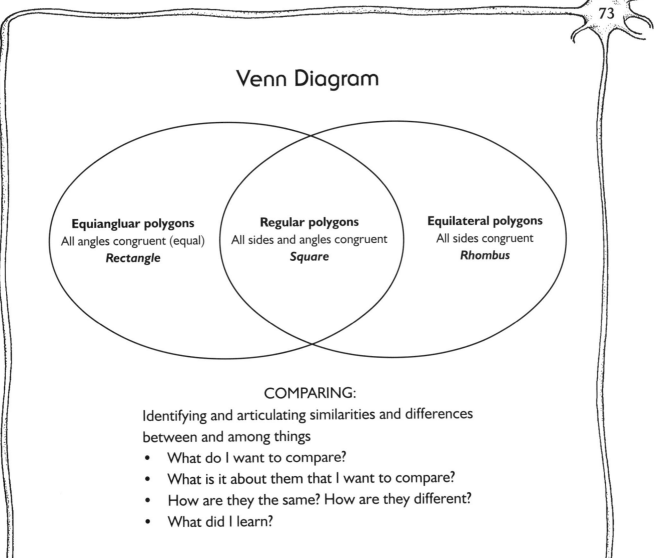

Equiangluar polygons
All angles congruent (equal)
Rectangle

Regular polygons
All sides and angles congruent
Square

Equilateral polygons
All sides congruent
Rhombus

COMPARING:

Identifying and articulating similarities and differences between and among things

- What do I want to compare?
- What is it about them that I want to compare?
- How are they the same? How are they different?
- What did I learn?

Figure 5.4

The more organized the material is, the more clearly its organization is perceived by the learner, and the greater the learning. Graphic organizers enable visual and spatial learners to "see" what they're thinking. The Math Strategy Graphic Organizer is an example of this kind of visual representation (see figure 5.5).

Patterning

The human brain's innate search for meaning occurs through "patterning," and it is through patterning that the brain seeks to achieve order from disorder. Such patterning would include schematic maps and categories, both

74

MATH STRATEGY
GRAPHIC ORGANIZER

Name: _____ Section: _____ Date: _____

1. Restate the question in your own words.

_____
_____
_____
_____

2. List the facts you will need to solve the problem.

- _____
- _____
- _____
- _____

- _____
- _____
- _____
- _____

3. Plan your strategy.

Step A: _____
Step B: _____
Step C: _____

4. Solve the problem:

Step A	Step B	Step C

5. Check: Does your answer make sense?

6. Answer

Figure 5.5

acquired and innate. The brain needs and automatically registers the familiar while simultaneously searching for and responding to novel stimuli. In other words the brain attempts to recognize and understand patterns as they occur and to give expression to unique and creative patterns of its own. An individual's brain has difficulty assimilating isolated bits of unrelated information that makes no sense to that individual. Use of the problem-solving strategies discussed in this chapter helps students learn effective techniques to create order out of what may at first seem chaotic. Such strategies enable learners to set up their own ordered systems for relevance, and therefore work well with the brain's innate search for order and meaning.

Current educational assessment practices were developed prior to the recent strides in the comprehension of brain learning, and therefore reflect society's beliefs about what is educationally important rather than a biological understanding of the brain's capabilities and limitations. Since some form of assessment is needed to ascertain curriculum effectiveness and student achievement, we need to rethink some of our traditional assessment methodologies. Is precise quantitative measurement important in everything? Learning consists of how our brain acquires information, and memory deals with how and where our brain stores this information. Factual memories are the principal element of school assessment programs; however, for factual information to be useful, our brain must connect it to its environmental setting and emotional challenge.

Project units provide useful emotional contexts because they are related to the real-life emotional uses of such information. Multiple-choice and other traditional assessment formats generally mask the context of factual information and usually result in an inability to recall such knowledge when it is needed in a real-life situation. Performance assessments that employ rubric evaluations, such as those in the next chapter, enhance the development of personal meaning and make the assessment a part of the leaning process. These performance assessments and rubric evaluations provide a more valid measure of the learned knowledge, which now can be used and applied in new and different situations.

CHAPTER 6

TEACHING AND ASSESSING WITH THE RUBRIC

A rubric implies that a rule defining the criteria of an assessment system is followed in an evaluation. A rubric can be an explicit description of performance characteristics corresponding to a point on a rating scale. A scoring rubric makes explicit expected qualities of performance on a rating scale or the definition of a single scoring point on a scale.

—The Building Tool Room 1995

While current educational assessment practices reflect society's beliefs about what is educationally important, they do not take into account the brain's capabilities or limitations. Assessments that were developed prior to recent brain research discoveries and understandings now appear to be less reliable and valid than once thought. Multiple-choice and other traditional assessment formats actually separate the context of factual information and make it seem irrelevant and unconnected, and are difficult for the brain to process for future use or store in long-term memory. In contrast, performance assessments that employ rubric evaluations encourage the development of personal meaning for the learner and relate the assessment aspect to the rest of the learning process. Performance assessments and rubric evaluations offer a new approach and can provide a valid measure of knowledge learned, since such assessments keep the information in context and allow the brain to organize such knowledge for application in new and different situations.

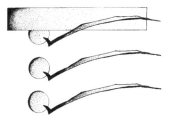

Scoring Rubrics

A rubric provides specific descriptions of what a performance or a product looks like at several different levels of quality. It acts as a guide providing direction to the scoring of student products and/or performances. It is especially helpful for assessing such products as open-ended questions, project work, visual representations, oral presentations, and written work. Usually presented in chart form, a rubric describes the various levels of work performance. A scoring rubric consists of

- a fixed scale (e.g., 4 points),
- a description of the characteristics for each of the points, and
- sample responses (anchors) which illustrate each point.

A rubric describes specific characteristics to look for when assessing each performance level. It can also help teachers visualize what the final version of an assignment will look like as well as encourage teachers to determine specifically what is expected at performance levels other than the "excellent" level. Rubrics encourage teachers to reflect on the validity and value of assignments before they are assigned as well as after they are completed.

Rubrics are equally important to both teachers and students. By clearly defining what is necessary for attainment of a particular level of performance, rubrics take the guesswork out of trying to understand what the teacher wants and expects. Rubrics enable students to set up definite goals as they approach their tasks. By setting specific goals, students begin to take ownership of their learning. Such empowerment raises student confidence, which results in a higher level of student performance.

Rubric standards, however, cannot be clearly identified without specific examples of student work to demonstrate what each of the "benchmark" standard levels represents. It is only through viewing these different levels of student work that learners experience how those standards are applied. These so-called benchmark rubrics are the guidelines students will use to measure their own work. By matching the evidence (student work) to a specific descriptor (benchmark and standard level), evaluations become more consistent, valid, and reliable and less subjective in nature.

Categories for Rubrics

Rubrics are usually divided into categories of either three, four, five, or six different levels of student work. The four-level rubric system is used in this book. According to Thomas Guskey, Professor of Educational Policy Studies and Evaluation at the University of Kentucky, "The more categories there are for grading, the greater the degree of subjectivity" (1997). A system with only three descriptors does not have enough sophistication to achieve an adequate differentiation among the different levels, while systems having five or more descriptors are likely to result in a more subjective evaluation.

Following is a list of descriptors on the developmental continuum:

1. Advanced: extended/sophisticated
- solution demonstrates an in-depth understanding
- demonstration of the ability to identify the appropriate mathematical concepts as well as necessary information
- use of a sophisticated and efficient strategy
- employment of complex reasoning
- clear, precise, detailed, step-by-step explanation
- mathematical representation actively used as a means of communicating ideas related to solution of the problem
- precise and appropriate use of mathematical terminology and notation

Advanced Level: Being able to generalize from previous mathematical experience, the student successfully experiments to create multiple solutions with a sophisticated and complex elaboration of the strategy used.

2. Proficient: satisfactory/adequate
- solution demonstrates an understanding of the problem and the most important concepts
- use of an appropriate strategy that leads to a solution
- mathematical procedures correctly and appropriately used
- clear explanation of the solution
- effective use of mathematical terminology and notation

Proficient Level: Understanding the problem, the student uses equations and strategies appropriately to arrive at a correct solution.

3. Basic: partial/elementary
- incomplete solution (only a partial understanding of the problem)
- employment of a strategy that is only partially useful
- some evidence of mathematical reasoning
- incomplete explanation or use of mathematical procedures
- partial use of appropriate mathematical terminology

Basic Level: Showing some awareness of the problem, the student attempts to use equations, but with a weak strategy and an incorrect solution.

4. Novice: beginning/minimal
- inappropriate concepts or procedures used
- solution has no relation to the task
- no evidence of a strategy or procedure
- no explanation of the solution
- no use or inappropriate use of mathematical representations (figures, diagrams, graphs, tables, etc.)

Novice Level: Having only a limited awareness of the problem, the student attempts the work without any strategy or organization.

These developmental levels can be used to form a rubric. The following rubric (figure 6.1) should serve as a guide for a four-category system of evaluation.

RUBRIC FOR PROGRESS ASSESSMENT

Advanced (Extended/Sophisticated)

- is able to make generalizations from previous mathematical experience
- successfully experiments to create multiple solutions
- sophisticated, complex, and detailed explanation of process, strategy, or strategies used

Proficient (Satisfactory/Adequate)

- demonstrates good comprehension of problem
- demonstrates a knowledge of appropriate equations and correct solutions
- able to describe strategy

Basic (Elementary/Partial)

- demonstrates some awareness and comprehension of problem
- weak, disorganized explanation of strategy
- equations are attempted, but most of solution is incorrect

Novice (Beginning/Minimal)

- demonstrates limited awareness and poor assessment of problem
- disorganized approach to problem
- no clear strategy or plan

Figure 6.1

The language of rubrics is important. Descriptors must be specific and contain enough detail so students can use the rubric as a guide when completing the assignments. They must be specific enough so both parents and students can clearly understand how those assignments will be evaluated. The descriptors must correlate with one another from one level to the next. If a particular characteristic is mentioned at one of the rubric levels, it must also be included at the other levels as well (see figure 6.2).

Listed below are a variety of performance descriptors. There is no limit to the number of possible words one can employ, but all descriptors must be used consistently so that students can develop an understanding of what the descriptors represent.

1. *Advanced* (Extended): sophisticated, awesome, exceptional, outstanding, exemplary achievement
2. *Proficient* (Adequate): satisfactory, admirable, effective, adequate understanding, commendable achievement
3. *Basic* (Elementary): partial, acceptable, limited understanding, limited evidence of achievement
4. *Novice* (Beginning): amateur, little or no understanding, minimal or no evidence of achievement

Types of Rubrics

There are many different kinds of rubrics. Some rubrics are designed to assess work for specific subjects or one particular assignment. These are generally referred to as subject-specific and task-specific rubrics. Other rubrics are more general and can be used in a variety of situations. Still other rubrics are used to assess student attitudes and behaviors such as how well students work in a cooperative group.

In March 1992 the U.S. Department of Labor published a report from the Secretary's Commission on Achieving Necessary Skills (SCANS). The report identified and described five separate skills and competencies needed for a successful work force that would ensure effective job performance in the twenty-first century:

1. *Resources:* student can identify, organize, plan, and allocate resources.

A RUBRIC FOR GROUP PROJECT PRESENTATIONS

Advanced (Extended)	Proficient (Adequate)	Basic (Elementary)	Novice (Beginning)
ORGANIZATION • well organized • logical format • excellent transitions from idea to idea	• thoughtfully organized • usually easy to follow • transitions easy to follow, but at times ideas unclear	• somewhat organized • somewhat incoherent • transitions not always smooth and at times distracted the audience	• choppy and confusing • difficult to follow • transitions were abrupt and distracted audience
COOPERATION • worked extremely well with each other • solicited, respected, and complemented others' ideas • highly productive	• worked very well with others • worked to get everyone involved • quite productive	• attempted to work well with others • at times "off task" and not everyone was actively involved • fairly productive	• did not work well with others • did not respect each other's opinions • argued often • showed little or no teamwork • unproductive
CONTENT • excellent job of research • utilized information effectively • sophisticated work level	• good job of research • utilized information in an efficient manner • satisfactory work level	• acceptable job of research • gathered limited information • limited work level	• minimal job of research • did little or no fact gathering • minimal work level
PRESENTATION • original, unique approach • engaging, provocative	• clever, at times unique • well done, interesting	• few original touches • at times interesting	• predictable, bland • did not keep audience interested

Figure 6.2

2. *Interpersonal:* student can work with others, lead, negotiate, and communicate.

3. *Information:* student can acquire, organize, interpret, and use information.

4. *Systems:* student can understand, monitor, and improve complex systems.

5. *Technology:* student can select, apply, and maintain a variety of technologies.

In its report, the Labor Department emphasized the importance of developing positive attitudes and working and communicating with others. Such interpersonal or attitudinal skills need to be taught in school. A Rubric for Group Project Presentations (see figure 6.2) can be used by students to self-assess how well their groups cooperate.

To produce a rubric, the assessment purpose must be precisely stated, so that the specific details needed for the rubric can be determined. The precise delineation of what students are expected to do must be generated as well as the types of learning (observable skills, products, or behaviors). There are two main purposes for assessment: (1) to identify which students have mastered an explicit instruction, or (2) to find student diagnostic information. In the first type of assessment, only two conclusions are possible: mastery or non-mastery. This is called *holistic scoring.*

A holistic rubric is used to assess the product by placing importance on the complete learning experience and on the ways in which the separate parts of that learning experience have been integrated. An example of a holistic rubric is the Thoughtful Outcomes Assessment (see figure 6.3). In this type of assessment, essential outcomes are assessed by having the student as well as the teacher make a list of what constitutes evidence of outcome achievement. The teacher reads the student's self-assessment, writes his or her own evaluation, and then determines the final grade.

When looking at diagnostic information, many variations in performance are possible. In this case, *analytic scoring* is used: the evaluator scores each performance on different, specific task elements, and the overall performance is the combination of the elements. Analytic rubrics target specific skills such as the level of content or the organizational skills of a group in its presentation of a project.

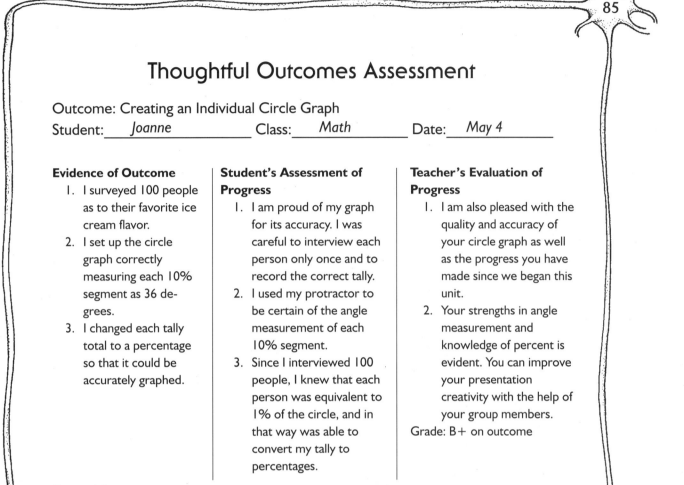

Thoughtful Outcomes Assessment

Outcome: Creating an Individual Circle Graph
Student: _Joanne_   Class: _Math_   Date: _May 4_

Evidence of Outcome

1. I surveyed 100 people as to their favorite ice cream flavor.
2. I set up the circle graph correctly measuring each 10% segment as 36 degrees.
3. I changed each tally total to a percentage so that it could be accurately graphed.

Student's Assessment of Progress

1. I am proud of my graph for its accuracy. I was careful to interview each person only once and to record the correct tally.
2. I used my protractor to be certain of the angle measurement of each 10% segment.
3. Since I interviewed 100 people, I knew that each person was equivalent to 1% of the circle, and in that way was able to convert my tally to percentages.

Teacher's Evaluation of Progress

1. I am also pleased with the quality and accuracy of your circle graph as well as the progress you have made since we began this unit.
2. Your strengths in angle measurement and knowledge of percent is evident. You can improve your presentation creativity with the help of your group members.

Grade: B+ on outcome

Figure 6.3

In summation, evaluation criteria for student assessment systems must rely upon the following concepts:

1. Standards specifying what students should know and be able to do are clearly defined before the assessment system is either developed or implemented.
2. The primary purpose of the assessment system is that of instruction and improvement in student learning.
3. The assessment standards, tasks, procedures, and uses are fair for all students.
4. The assessment tasks are varied and appropriately reflect the standards students are expected to achieve.
5. The assessment procedures and results are easy to understand.

6. There is enough flexibility programmed into the assessment system so that it has the ability to evolve and adapt to changing conditions.

7. The assessment results are only one part of a system of multiple indicators of educational quality. (Other indicators may be community profile, resources, programs, etc.)

8. The teachers participate in the design, administration, scoring, and use of the assessment tests.

(For additional examples of self-assessment rubrics, see figures 6.4 and 6.5.)

Brain-Compatible Assessment

Rubrics, or performance assessment scoring guides, have vital functions in assessment. They serve as tools that help the evaluator assign values to a given assessment. The kind of scoring rubric chosen depends upon the use for which that rubric was intended. The more precisely the purpose of the assessment is stated, the easier it is to construct a scoring guide or rubric. The following concepts must be kept in mind when designing a rubric:

- set clear assignment standards for the interpretation of student work, and
- determine the levels of rubric scoring that are applicable to the processes, skills, content, and attitudes.

Multiple-choice and other traditional assessment formats isolate information into unconnected bits and pieces taken out of context. The brain views this separation of content from context as fragmented information, both irrelevant and unconnected. These unrelated units of information are difficult for the brain to process for future use or store in long-term memory since they seem unrelated to any prior knowledge that the brain might use to make connections. On the other hand, performance assessments that employ rubric evaluations enhance the brain's ability to find connections and encourage the development of personal meaning for the learner.

The next chapter targets the portfolio as being one of the most desirable methods of performance assessment in terms of providing a detailed and accurate profile of an individual's growth and progress over an extended period of time.

SELF-ASSESSMENT FOR COOPERATIVE GROUP WORK

On a scale of 1 to 4 rate your group's success in working together.

4 = EXCELLENT   3 = GOOD   2 = ADEQUATE   1 = POOR

1.	Keeping to realistic goal plans	4	3	2	1
2.	Organizing the work as a team	4	3	2	1
3.	Carrying out individual group roles	4	3	2	1
4.	Accepting individual responsibility	4	3	2	1
5.	Listening to each other respectfully	4	3	2	1
6.	Waiting for each other's turn to speak	4	3	2	1
7.	Encouraging each other	4	3	2	1
8.	Discouraging "put-downs"	4	3	2	1

For the most part I think our group_____

_____

_____

_____

_____

_____

_____

_____

_____

_____

_____

Name:_____   Date: _____

Section: _____

Figure 6.4

GENERIC OUTLINE FOR STUDENT SELF-ASSESSMENT

Name:_____ Section:_____ Date:_____

How to Grade the Project:

- Were all project objectives and criteria met? Were they accurate?
- Were all written aspects of this project done well (correct spelling and sentence structure; neat and organized)?

Superior: (E)

_____ my work was superior/excellent
_____ I made many positive contributions to the group effort in every way possible
_____ I encouraged other members and assisted them whenever they needed help
_____ I was key to my group's success

Satisfactory: (S)

_____ my work was complete and correct
_____ I made several positive contributions to the group effort
_____ I encouraged at least one group member
_____ I helped my group succeed

Unsatisfactory: (U)

_____ I could have done better
_____ I did not encourage others
_____ I did not worry about my group
_____ I kind of goofed off

Explain the reasons for the grade you gave in four or five complete sentences. Which group members were most helpful? Which were not?

1. What new concepts did you learn from doing this project?

2. Did you find any part of this project difficult? If so, which part?

3. Was there any part of the project which you liked best? Why?

4. What did you enjoy or not enjoy about working with your teammates for this project?

5. Do you prefer to work in groups of 2, 3, or 4? Why?

6. How do you feel about our class right now?

7. What do you think we can we do to improve this class?

Figure 6.5

SkyLight Training and Publishing Inc.

CHAPTER 7

TEACHING AND ASSESSING WITH THE PORTFOLIO

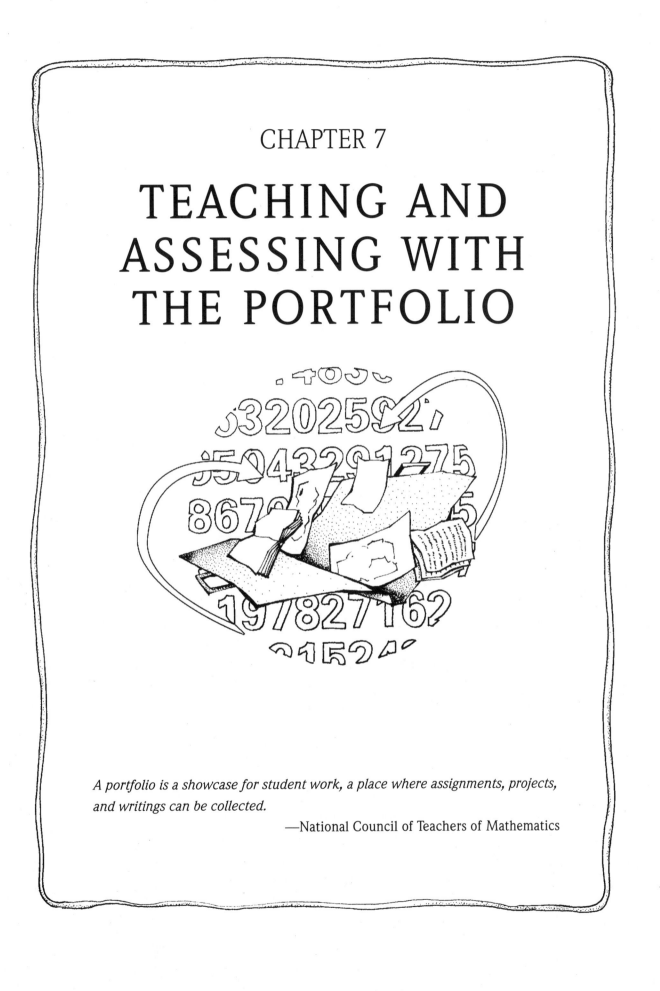

A portfolio is a showcase for student work, a place where assignments, projects, and writings can be collected.

—National Council of Teachers of Mathematics

While traditional assessment formats, such as multiple-choice unit tests, take information out of its relevant context and segment it into unconnected bits and pieces, authentic assessment does not. With authentic assessment, the evaluation occurs within a contextual setting that reflects the relevancy and integration of the subject matter. The separation of content from context that is characteristic of traditional assessment formats causes the brain to view such fragmented information as irrelevant and unconnected. These unrelated units of information are difficult for the brain to process for future use or store in long-term memory since they seem unrelated to any prior knowledge the brain might use to make connections. Performance assessments, on the other hand, employ rubric evaluations that enhance the brain's ability to find connections and encourage the development of personal meaning for the learner.

Student Evaluation

Among different performance assessments, the portfolio stands out as one of the most comprehensive forms of student evaluation: it visually captures the learning process while demonstrating the growth that students will experience over an extended period of time. It allows for the documentation and evaluation of student work, and enables the teacher and student to work together in compiling both formal and informal examples of learning.

The development of a portfolio for assessment purposes requires planning and effort, since the portfolio is much more than a compilation of tests and papers. Students need additional instruction in order to deal with a new and different kind of assessment, and teachers need to use new and different implementation strategies in order to help the students learn to work with such an assessment system.

The portfolio's purpose is to capture a series of "learning snapshots" that can provide an ongoing history of each student's growth throughout the year. The projects and reflections included in the portfolio illuminate the curriculum areas being studied. The portfolio is both product as well as process. It is an organized, purposeful collection of documents, artifacts, records of achievement, and reflections. It is also the process of gathering, organizing, and using the documents and experiences to demonstrate the learning, instruction, and growth that have transpired.

A portfolio usually consists of

- a table of contents written by the student,
- artifacts (the evidence of what learning has occurred—the student's work),
- captions (explanations written by the student for each item contained in the portfolio), and
- reflections on the learning, as well as group and self-evaluations written by the student.

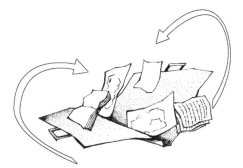

Portfolio Assessment

There is strong evidence supporting the need for performance assessment at all levels of education. Portfolios and portfolio assessment provide evaluators with opportunities to evaluate the multiple facets of student growth and development that have always been difficult to assess using traditional assessment formats. Portfolios are unique in that they

- illustrate a student's progress and growth over time,
- demonstrate that significant learning is occurring—through evidence that addresses such growth and development across the curriculum,
- allow parents to see and value their children's progress,
- encourage parents to become partners in their children's education and become more aware of the curriculum their children learn,
- enable the teacher to become more knowledgeable about each student's individual strengths and weaknesses, and
- value process as well as product.

Portfolios help to develop higher-order thinking strategies such as analysis, synthesis, and evaluation. Analysis is the breaking down of a concept or a series of concepts into its constituent parts; synthesis is the combining of the constituent elements into a single entity; and evaluation is the process whereby set standards are used to judge the quality of the components.

Thus, the portfolio experience revolutionizes the current educational grading model by having the student monitor his or her own learning. With the portfolio process, evaluation is internalized, and it is this metacognitive internalization of the self-evaluation process that is one of the most important skills a person can learn.

A Portfolio System

The job of establishing a system of portfolio evaluation can at times seem overwhelming to the teacher since the format is so different from traditional assessment modalities. However, new instructional methods require different forms of evaluation. If educators are to employ performance-based instruction using performance tasks, it must follow that they will need performance-based assessments to evaluate with any modicum of validity. The portfolio provides one of the most comprehensive tools for such performance assessment.

To ease the educator's transition from the traditional unit test evaluation to the more effective and relevant portfolio-style evaluation, this chapter provides numerous classroom-ready portfolio items for use in different situations (see figures 7.1–7.10). These outlines, evaluations, and reflective guides provide alternatives to those provided in the project units contained in section 2 of this book. There are letters for both students and for parents introducing this unique and possibly unfamiliar format (see figures 7.1 and 7.2). Other items include a form for students to use to track the items in their portfolios (see figure 7.4), a rubric for portfolio assessment (see figure 7.7), and a black-line master of the Math Strategy Graphic Organizer (see figure 5.5).

Section 1 of this book has provided a background and rationale for the use of brain-compatible learning strategies in the contemporary mathematics classroom. Through the use of brain imaging techniques, new scientific data can offer insight into which instructional strategies are most in keeping with the brain's natural method of processing, learning, and storing information. Section 2 of this book presents classroom-ready integrated mathematic project units that encourage such connections, contextual applications, and meaningful learning.

PORTFOLIO LETTER TO STUDENTS

Dear Students:

Please share this letter with your parents and guardians.

This year you will be completing a portfolio for each quarter that will provide evidence of mastery of the learning goals and objectives related to specific units of our math work. Your portfolio may contain assignments, tests, projects, reports or activities that demonstrate your knowledge and understanding. Along with samples of your work, your portfolio should also contain

- a *table of contents* that will serve as a "guide" through the portfolio,

- a *caption* or paragraph attached to each piece of work explaining why you have chosen it as evidence of your achievement, and

- a *reflection* or conclusion stating your personal reactions to each of the selected pieces.

As a final check of the finished portfolio, ask yourself the following questions:

1. Is my portfolio well organized?

2. Have I included sample evidence for each and every learning goal?

3. Is the connection between each piece of evidence and the learning goal obvious?

4. Does each piece of evidence in my portfolio add to its value and make it better?

Although it takes time, effort, and thought to construct a portfolio, this kind of evaluation also allows for the expression of your creativity and individuality. I challenge you to make your portfolio special and unique. I look forward to viewing the finished products.

Figure 7.1

PARENT PORTFOLIO REVIEW & REFLECTION

Student:_____ Reader:_____ Date:_____

Student self-assessment is a dynamic and powerful instructional tool. As a learning tool, it is effective because it helps the students

- develop responsibility for their own learning,
- become motivated for improvement,
- internalize criteria for success,
- learn to use assessment for growth, and
- think reflectively.

The performance assessment processes used in this class employ both student and teacher input. These processes use observations and judgments to evaluate student performance, based on clearly defined criteria. We invite you to be part of this performance assessment process.

Please look over and read everything in your child's portfolio. Each piece is accompanied by his/her performance assessment. The portfolios also include reflections and self-evaluations.

When you have read the portfolio, please talk to your child about the work. The following questions can help guide you in the discussion.

Which piece(s) of work in the portfolio tells you the most about his/her critical thinking or problem-solving skills? _____

_____

What does it tell you? _____

_____

What do you see as the strengths in your child's thinking skills?_____

_____

What do you think needs to be addressed in your child's growth and development?

_____

_____

Other comments, suggestions _____

_____

_____

Thank you so much for investing the time in your child's education!

Figure 7.2

INSIDE YOUR PORTFOLIO: SOME SUGGESTIONS

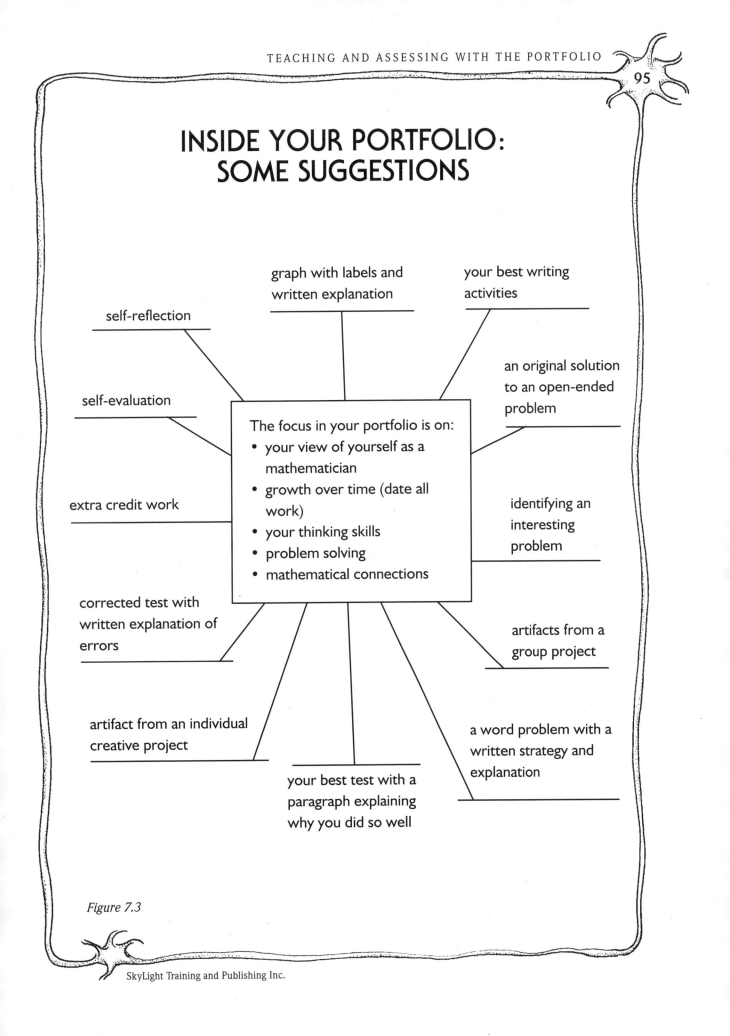

graph with labels and written explanation

your best writing activities

self-reflection

an original solution to an open-ended problem

self-evaluation

The focus in your portfolio is on:
- your view of yourself as a mathematician
- growth over time (date all work)
- your thinking skills
- problem solving
- mathematical connections

extra credit work

identifying an interesting problem

corrected test with written explanation of errors

artifacts from a group project

artifact from an individual creative project

a word problem with a written strategy and explanation

your best test with a paragraph explaining why you did so well

Figure 7.3

SkyLight Training and Publishing Inc.

PORTFOLIO CONTENTS
PERSONAL TRACKING FORM

Name: _____

Date M	D	Title	Shared With	Problem Solving	Reflection	Basic Skills	Collaboration

Figure 7.4

REFLECTIONS FOR INDIVIDUAL PORTFOLIO ENTRY

Name:_____ Section:_____ Date:_____

This is my favorite piece because:_____
_____
_____
_____
_____
_____
_____

The new math concepts I have learned from this activity are:_____
_____
_____
_____
_____
_____
_____

If I could do this piece over again, I would: _____
_____
_____
_____
_____
_____
_____

I like (dislike) the idea of a portfolio because:_____
_____
_____
_____
_____
_____
_____
_____
_____
_____

Figure 7.5

SkyLight Training and Publishing Inc.

PORTFOLIO REFLECTION SHEET

Name: _____

Section: _____

Title: _____

Entry date: _____

Focus: Identify the primary category focus for this portfolio entry. Is it:

❑ PROBLEM-SOLVING ?   ❑ REFLECTION ?   ❑ BASIC SKILLS?   ❑ COLLABORATION?

Describe your entry . . .

What is your entry about? _____
_____
_____

Why did you chose this as an entry? _____
_____
_____

What did you learn from this activity? _____
_____
_____
_____
_____
_____
_____
_____
_____
_____
_____
_____
_____
_____

Figure 7.6

PORTFOLIO EVALUATION RUBRIC

Name: _____

Evaluated by: _____

	ADVANCED	PROFICIENT	BASIC	NOVICE
Presentation	• exciting to look at	• attractive presentation	• some parts are pleasing to look at	• little effort put into display of work
Variety	• contains a wide variety of work	• contains some variety of work	• contains little variety of work	• contains no variety of work
Organization	• clearly organized	• organized	• somewhat organized	• disorganized
Communication	• clear communication of ideas	• some ideas communicated clearly	• few ideas communicated clearly	• no ideas communicated clearly
Understanding	• shows exceptional understanding	• shows some understanding	• shows little understanding	• shows no understanding
Self-Assessment	• evidence of thorough, realistic, and constructive self-assessment	• evidence of some realistic self-assessment	• little evidence of realistic self-assessment	• self-assessment does not correspond to performance

Figure 7.7

STUDENT PORTFOLIO ASSESSMENT – A

Name:_____ Section:_____ Date:_____

1. What are the new concepts you have learned, and how does your portfolio demonstrate this new learning?_____
_____
_____
_____
_____
_____

2. Specifically, what did you learn about these new concepts? (What new under-standings about math did you gain that you didn't have before?)_____
_____
_____
_____

3. What would you like to finish or do over again now that you have learned these new concepts?_____
_____
_____
_____

4. Has your writing in math class improved since the beginning of the year, and if so, how has it improved? _____
_____
_____
_____

5. When you don't understand new work, what do you do to help yourself under-stand it better? _____
_____
_____
_____

6. Do you do the same thing when you are having trouble with your project work, and if you don't, what do you do to help yourself? _____
_____
_____
_____

Figure 7.8

SkyLight Training and Publishing Inc.

STUDENT PORTFOLIO ASSESSMENT – B

Name:_____   Section:_____   Date:_____

1. Concepts, procedures, relationships explored _____
   _____
   _____
   _____
   _____

2. Areas of growth in understanding _____
   _____
   _____
   _____
   _____

3. Unfinished work or work needing revision _____
   _____
   _____
   _____
   _____

4. Assessment of the following areas:
   a. Problem-solving work
      _____
      _____
      _____

   b. Reasoning and critical thinking
      _____
      _____
      _____

   c. Writing in math
      _____
      _____
      _____

   d. Other
      _____
      _____
      _____

Figure 7.9

SkyLight Training and Publishing Inc.

SECTION II

SAMPLE UNIT TASKS

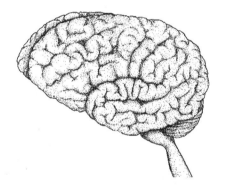

INTRODUCTION

Brain-Based Learning: The Rationale for
Project Unit Tasks

The units in section 2 of this book appeal to the multiple intelligences in different combinations. Chapter 8 addresses the primary/elementary level. The task "Shapes, Patterns, and Tessellations" appeals to linguistic intelligence through the discussion and reflective activities that are included throughout this unit task (as well as all the others); the logical/mathematical as well as spatial components for this task are the aspects dealing with the geometry of the shapes; and the socialization aspect of team pairing supports interpersonal intelligence.

In "Project: Party!" linguistic and interpersonal intelligences are affected in much the same way as they were in the previous unit task. The logical/mathematical component in this task, however, uses the learner's curiosity about money and finance as a means for motivation and also makes use of a bodily-kinesthetic approach in that the physical aspect of purchasing items has been integrated into the task as well. "Candy-Counter Mathematics" appeals to the linguistic, logical-mathematical, and interpersonal intelligences much in the same way as the previous two tasks have done.

Chapter 9 addresses the higher elementary-middle level. The first unit, entitled "Money, Graphs, and All That Jazz!," appeals to linguistic, logical-mathematical, spatial, bodily-kinesthetic, interpersonal, and intrapersonal intelligences. At this level, the linguistic component involves individual reflective writings as well as group discussions. The mathematics have become more sophisticated, and intrapersonal intelligence has been added, being fostered through metacognitive activities such as individual and group reflections. The unit entitled "How Do Your Genes Fit?" appeals to linguistic, logical-mathematical, spatial, bodily-kinesthetic, interpersonal, and intrapersonal intelligences much in the same way.

Chapter 10 addresses the secondary level. The unit "Home Improvement" appeals to linguistic, logical-mathematical, spatial, bodily-kinesthetic, interpersonal, and intrapersonal intelligences at a secondary level of challenge and sophistication.

Each of the included units and lessons employs the brain-compatible teaching and learning approaches discussed in section 1. The activities in section 2 also expand on performance-based instructional strategies and problem-solving techniques, and show examples of rubrics in action.

Renate and Geoffrey Caine (1994) organized the educational paradigm shift towards brain-based learning into a framework based on the following twelve principles, which they called brain/mind learning principles:

1. The brain is a complex, adaptive system.
2. The brain is a social brain.
3. The search for meaning is innate.
4. The search for meaning occurs through "patterning."
5. Emotions are critical to patterning.
6. Every brain simultaneously perceives and creates parts and wholes.
7. Learning involves both focused attention and peripheral perception.
8. Learning always involves conscious and unconscious processes.
9. We have at least two ways of organizing memory.
10. Learning is developmental.
11. Complex learning is enhanced by challenge and inhibited by threat.
12. Every brain is uniquely organized.

With these twelve brain principles we move away from the view of the learner as a blank slate and also avoid the natural tendency to segment the learner into separate cognitive, emotional, or physical functions. Each of the project-units that follow incorporates these brain-based principles.

In applying the concepts of brain-based learning to the business of education, students are encouraged to learn in a challenging and content-rich environment through the use of project unit tasks. At the same time, this challenging environment must also foster a sense of safety and trust. Students must feel physically as well as emotionally "safe" enough to explore, conjecture, and experiment with innovative and nontraditional solutions to those problems being posed in the project units. Such project-centered instruction is academically powerful because it enhances learning and assessment in unique ways. Projects require self-directed learning, synthesis of information, in-depth analysis, problem solving, and persistence.

In a classroom where the learning environment has been designed to be brain-compatible, students are offered the kinds of learning experiences that teach knowledge organization, information synthesis, the reinforcement of self-correction skills, and concept application. These learning experiences both demonstrate and employ the contextual application of new knowledge much the way it occurs in real life, thereby imbuing the learning with relevancy and connection to the world outside the classroom.

The best way to assess performance project tasks is with rubrics that incorporate assessment of research, content learning, key concepts, communication skills (both oral and written), and types of thinking (creative and original). Performance assessments that use rubrics are closely tied to the curriculum; because such assessments value depth of understanding over shallow coverage, they can reveal much more about students' learning than standardized multiple-choice tests.

In the project-task suggestions that follow, the mathematical content is presented in a manner that attempts to simulate each task's authentic contextual setting. Mathematical concept instruction is much more brain-compatible when the applications of those concepts occur as natural extensions of experiential learning rather than compartmentalized textbook presentations. In this way the responsibility for the learning shifts directly to the students as they develop their own comprehension of underlying mathematic concepts—an enduring comprehension that stays with them throughout their lifetime.

Brain-compatible learning focuses on solutions to mathematical problems that require reasoning rather than the repetitious practice of algorithms. While all students should meet rigorous mathematical standards, some may, indeed, need to achieve these goals through different and perhaps unconventional means.

Through the use of project units, students will come to realize that mathematics is not a discipline based strictly on a set of rules understood by only a few, but rather that mathematical comprehension is an evolving process for all involving exploration, conjecture, and logical reasoning.

CHAPTER 8

PRIMARY AND ELEMENTARY LEVEL TASKS

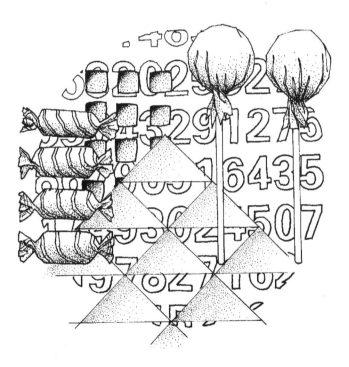

Chapter 8 contains lessons appropriate for primary and lower elementary level students. Along with mathematics, the development of socialization and communication skills are of primary concern for this age group. The three units in this chapter emphasize the development of these important skills.

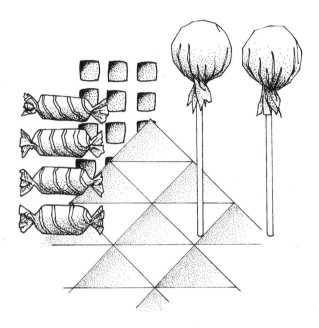

— UNIT ONE —

SHAPES, PATTERNS, AND TESSELLATIONS

Primary Level

This primary mathematics unit, "Shapes, Patterns, and Tessellations," studies geometric shapes and their occurrence in the world outside the classroom. A set of primary objectives for geometry is covered as well as introductory geometric vocabulary and terms.

In tasks 1 and 2, the students learn about geometric shapes and their tessellating qualities (the ability of geometric shapes to form a pattern design in which all the shapes touch, yet there are no empty spaces between the touching shapes). The students then progress to task 3 where they create original multishape tessellations on their own.

This unit follows the recommendations of Caine and Caine (1994) for implementation of brain-based learning in schools:

- It provides variety and stimulation.
- The students are creating designs (products) using their creative interests as the springboard.
- The "pair and share" model allows for individualized learning plans that are developed according to each student's learning style, assorted intelligences, strengths, interests, and needs.
- The community provides the resources for examples of geometry in the real world, as well as ideas for different geometry design and pattern extensions.
- The teacher acts in the capacity of a resource, facilitator, coach, and guide.

Following is a list of Caine and Caine's brain/mind learning principles as well as the manner in which this unit specifically implements these principles:

1. *The brain is a complex, adaptive system.* Students will adapt and learn in an environment that supports them by encouraging teamwork and pairing while challenging them to learn geometric concepts.
2. *The brain is a social brain.* Because socialization is natural for the brain, the beginnings of group learning are introduced in the "pair and share" format.
3. *The search for meaning is innate.* Students will look for the appearance and relevancy of geometry in their own world.
4. *The search for meaning occurs through "patterning."* Through the creation of their own geometry patterns and designs, students will be more in tune with geometric patterns in the world around them.
5. *Emotions are critical to patterning.* It is especially important at the primary level that the learning environment be challenging, exciting, and nonthreatening so that the process of new learning is a positive experience for these young children. Their natural curiosity will provide intrinsic motivation, and the security they experience through this nonthreatening modality makes their early mathematical experiences very positive ones.

6. *Every brain simultaneously perceives and creates parts and wholes.* Students will perceive the geometric shapes as individual entities as well as parts of a larger design.

7. *Learning involves both focused attention and peripheral perception.* While the young learners may be focused on their task, their teacher's attitude and enthusiasm about the lesson becomes an integral part of that learning experience.

8. *Learning always involves conscious and unconscious processes.* The students may focus on the geometric shapes and design construction, yet their brains will begin to search out connections to similar shapes in their everyday environment both inside and outside the classroom.

9. *We have at least two ways of organizing memory.* We have a set of systems for receiving relatively unrelated information. There is a part of our brains geared to rote memorization as well as a spatial/autobiographical memory that does not need rehearsal, and which allows for instant recall of experiences. This lesson involves the latter in that the visual and spatial recognition of the shapes enables the brain to develop a form of instant recall.

10. *Learning is developmental.* Geometry can be learned at any level of development. This particular unit is appropriate for young students.

11. *Complex learning is enhanced by challenge and inhibited by threat.* It is for this vital reason that the student's early learning experiences must be nonthreatening and enjoyable ones.

12. *Every brain is uniquely organized,* and as such, will interpret information and lesson directions in an individual manner, thereby encouraging the young learner to become increasingly self-confident and self-reliant.

The contextual learning in this unit is designed around the student's creative interests. All of the learning is structured around the recognition and knowledge of geometric shapes. The students work together in pairs. Learning and processing can take place outside the classroom as well as inside. Also, students have the opportunity to monitor their own learning as well as maximize that learning. Metacognitive opportunities are also encouraged through the use of self-evaluation (see figure 8.4).

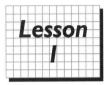

Lesson 1 — Shapes, Patterns, and Tessellations

Objectives

1. To encourage the exploration of the relationships between and among basic geometric shapes.
2. To encourage pattern recognition and creation through the use of simple geometric shapes.
3. To encourage the design and formation of individual, unique geometric patterns.

Materials

Pattern blocks, regular and colored pencils, paper

Vocabulary

1. *square:* a shape with four equal sides and each side at right angles
2. *triangle:* a three-sided shape
3. *tessellate:* shapes tessellate and form a tessellation design when all of the shapes in the design touch on all the sides, and there are no empty spaces between the shapes

Task 1

The teacher introduces the task with a discussion of what tessellations are, and where they can be found in the real world, for example, bathroom floors, kitchen walls and floors, ceiling tiles.

The students are then encouraged to work in pairs to create their own tessellation designs with the pattern blocks. Students will need guidance and frequent reminders that there cannot be any empty spaces if the shapes are to tessellate.

Task 2

Using two different kinds of pattern blocks, the teacher demonstrates how to trace (outline) the pattern block's shape. The students then practice tracing one of the shapes on their own. Once familiar with the tracing technique, the students can then design tessellation patterns of their own using a single geometric shape that tessellates (see figures 8.1 and 8.2).

Squares

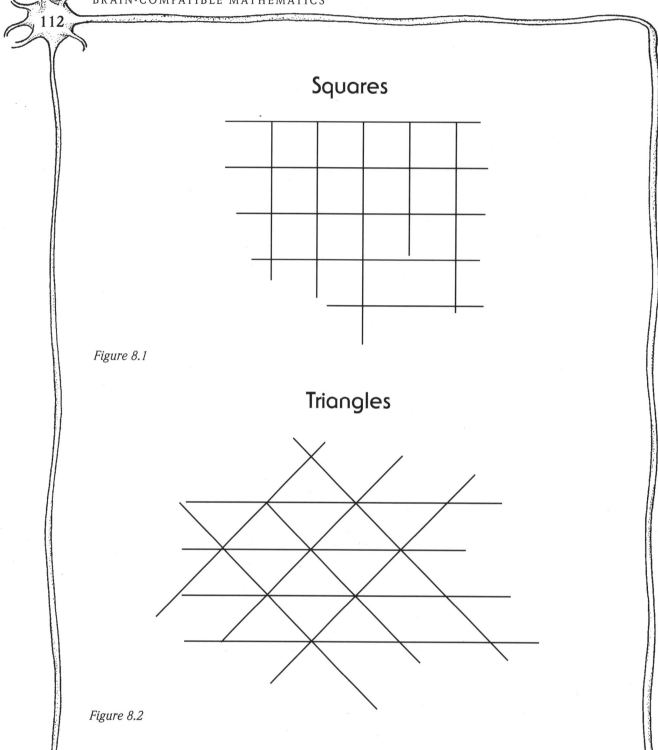

Figure 8.1

Triangles

Figure 8.2

Task 3

In the second, more advanced pattern design, the teacher demonstrates tessellation development (the building of pattern combinations). The students then experiment on their own with two shapes that tessellate (that is, the triangle and square). After the tessellation drawings have been completed, encourage the students to color their designs in intricate ways (see figure 8.3).

Squares and Triangles

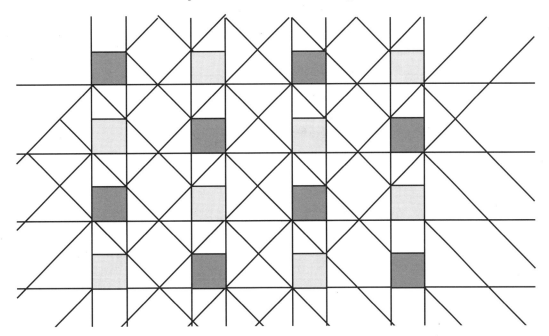

Figure 8.3

An example of a primary level student self-assessment can be found on the next page (see figure 8.4).

GEOMETRY TESSELLATION SELF-ASSESSMENT
Primary Grades

1. Did I follow the teacher's directions?

2. Do all of my shapes fit together?

3. Does my tessellation have any empty spaces?

4. Do all of my shapes form a pattern?

5. Can I make a tessellation design by myself now?

Figure 8.4

SkyLight Training and Publishing, Inc.

— UNIT TWO —

PROJECT: PARTY!

Elementary Level

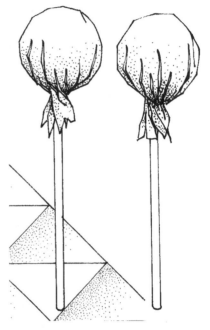

In the elementary mathematics lesson "Project: Party!," the students gain experience with money, finance, and budget planning. A set of elementary objectives is covered as well as basic monetary terminology.

In task 1 of this unit the student teams design and construct posters to help them understand and pictorially represent different monetary values. In tasks 2 and 3 the students plan a "budget" and work out the logistic and financial details involved in planning a real party. In task 4 the actual purchases are made, and the unit culminates in the reward of students enjoying the party itself. For help in organizing and presenting this unit, see the Problem Ladder Graphic Organizer (figure 8.5).

This unit also uses recommendations suggested by Caine and Caine (1994) for the implementation of brain-based learning in schools:

- It provides variety and stimulation.
- The students are creating products and experiencing new situations using their own interests and motivations as the springboard.
- The group (team) model allows for individualized learning plans that are developed according to each student's learning style, assorted intelligences, strengths, interests, and needs.
- The community provides the resources for actual purchasing experiences.
- The teacher acts in the capacity of a resource, facilitator, coach, and guide.

Following is a list of Caine and Caine's brain/mind learning principles and how this unit specifically implements them:

1. *The brain is a complex, adaptive system.* Students will adapt and learn in a supportive and challenging learning environment. Through the newly learned knowledge in finance, the students build confidence and raise their own awareness level of the world outside the classroom.

2. *The brain is a social brain.* For this reason, socialization and the dynamics of group learning are introduced as part of the unit objectives.

3. *The search for meaning is innate.* Students will look for the appearance and relevancy of concepts such as expenses and budgets in their own day-to-day experiences.

4. *The search for meaning occurs through "patterning."* By working with facsimile money through making a money-value poster, and in planning an actual party budget, students will see the pattern and logic to a monetary system.

5. *Emotions are critical to patterning.* It is important for the learning environment to be challenging, exciting, and nonthreatening so that learning can be a positive experience for young students.

6. *Every brain simultaneously perceives and creates parts and wholes.* Students will develop an understanding of monetary equivalencies as both parts (coin denominations) and wholes (dollar denominations).

7. *Learning involves both focused attention and peripheral perception.* While the students may be focused on their task, both the teacher's as well as their team members' attitudes toward the lesson become part of the learning experience. If the teacher treats the handling of finances as a matter of responsibility and importance, this attitude then carries over to the young learners.

8. *Learning always involves conscious and unconscious processes.* The students may focus on the party budget and expenses, yet their brains will begin to search out similar monetary concepts in their everyday environment both inside and outside the classroom.

9. *We have at least two ways of organizing memory.* We have a set of systems for receiving relatively unrelated information. There is a part

of our brains geared to rote memorization as well as a spatial/autobiographical memory that does not need rehearsal, and which allows for instant recall of experiences. This lesson involves both types of memory: rote learning of coin and currency equivalencies, and the connection and application of such monetary units to the act of purchasing goods.

10. *Learning is developmental.* Finances can be learned at any level of development. This particular unit involving the planning of a small party is appropriate for young learners since there is intrinsic motivation for the goal to be reached and the steps involved in the planning are simple ones.

11. *Complex learning is enhanced by challenge and inhibited by threat.* It is for this reason that it is important to make early learning experiences nonthreatening and enjoyable for students. Going outside the classroom to make the party purchases helps to build self-confidence and self-reliance in young learners.

12. *Every brain is uniquely organized,* and as such, will interpret information and lesson directions in an individual manner.

This unit's contextual learning is also specifically designed around student interests. All of the learning is structured around real issues and problems. The students work together in teams. The learning takes place outside the classroom as well as inside. Furthermore, students have the opportunity to monitor as well as maximize their own learning. Metacognitive opportunities are included in the unit to encourage self-reflection (see figure 8.6).

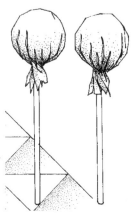

Lesson 2

Project: Party!

Objectives

1. To explore the concept of money and how finances work.
2. To develop the concepts of "equivalency" both kinesthetically and conceptually.
3. To develop group problem-solving skills and team dynamics.

Materials for poster

Colored construction paper, scissors, glue, colored pencils, markers

Vocabulary

1. *penny*
2. *nickel*
3. *dime*
4. *quarter*
5. *dollar*
6. *budget*
7. *expenses*
8. *supplies*

Task 1

Each team is responsible for the design and construction of a "money" poster. While each student makes a separate part of his or her team's money poster, they are responsible as a team unit for the final product's quality. The purpose of the poster is to display the team's knowledge of money as displayed in different denominations, for example, one dime = 10 pennies = 2 nickels and so forth.

The poster design and layout is up to the students in each of the teams, but coin and dollar equivalents up to $10.00 must be included.

Task 2

Once the students have become comfortable with the handling and concept of coin and currency value, the class is ready to plan "Project: Party!"   The first step in "Project: Party!" is to plan a budget as to the total amount of money the class will have to spend. The total amount is then divided among the four groups to create a "team budget." Next, each team works out the details as to what they will need in the way of party supplies. Each of the four teams is responsible for one of the four necessary party categories. Team A is in charge of drinks and beverages. Team B decides what kind and color of paper goods will be used at the party. Team C chooses the salty snack foods, and team D is in charge of the sweets.

To help them plan what kind of foods and party items to purchase, the class will take a trip to a local market where the students can do their research as a team. This research consists of identifying and comparing different items and brands. The teams need to keep track of the different items, as well as each item's cost, for the data analysis project component (task 3) back in the classroom.

Task 3

The teams are now ready to plan their purchases based on how much money they have in the team budget for their part of "Project: Party!" At this point, some teacher and team consultation time is to be scheduled so that the team can get feedback as to whether they are being reasonable as to their budget and their choices.

The agreed-upon amount of money is then collected within the teams, with each team coordinator in charge of collecting that group's money. The recorder keeps a list of who brought in what amount, and both the resource manager and the materials manager have the job of checking that the correct amount has been collected and credited.

Task 4

The class makes the actual purchasing trip to the store, but this time each team has a specific list of supplies to buy along with the anticipated cost of each item. The reward for all of this hard work, of course, is the party itself.

PROBLEM LADDER GRAPHIC ORGANIZER

Curriculum Area(s): _Mathematics_   Project Length: _1-2 weeks_

Performance Task Title: _Project: Party!_   Grade Level(s): _2-5_

Resources/Materials: _colored construction paper, scissors, glue, selected party supplies_

TASK DESCRIPTION

The students are divided into teams for the purpose of planning their own party. Each team has the responsibility of planning for one of the four major aspects of the party: paper goods, beverages, sweet snacks, and salty snacks. To help plan what they will buy, the students first take a data-gathering trip to a local market to learn about item cost and selection. Next, the teams decide what to purchase and how much to spend on each item, according to the established budget. After the items and amounts have been approved during the teacher and team meeting, the purchasing trip to the market is made, and the final step of the project is to enjoy the party.

PROJECT OBJECTIVES

Student comprehension of concepts

- _working with different financial denominations_

- _gathering and collating data_

- _organizing and planning an event_

Student skill and process development

- _money estimation and calculation_

- _introduction to decimals_

- _cost comparisons_

PRODUCTS AND/OR PERFORMANCES

Group Products

- _budget for team task_

- _tally of collected moneys_

- _final list of items to be purchased_

Individual Products

- _money poster_

- _record of money collected or check of money collected_

Extensions

- _help plan a class trip_

- _plan another event_

CRITERIA FOR PRODUCT EVALUATION

Group Products

- _Is the budget realistic?_

- _Is the money tally accurate?_

- _Is the final list of items reasonable?_

Individual Products

- _Is the money poster accurate?_

- _Are both the record of collections and the check of those collections accurate?_

Extensions

- _Is the new event doable?_

- _Can it work logistically?_

- _Can it work financially?_

Figure 8.5

SkyLight Training and Publishing, Inc.

PERFORMANCE TASK SELF-ASSESSMENT
Elementary Grades

1. Was my part of the group budget plans accurate and correct?

2. Was I helpful to team members during the project when they needed help?

3. Are all my numbers on the money poster correct and in the right order?

4. Is my purchasing research work correct? Does it make sense?

5. Can I now plan a shopping trip by myself? Can I work with a budget?

Figure 8.6

— UNIT THREE —

CANDY-COUNTER MATHEMATICS
Elementary Level

In the lesson for this unit the student teams are charged with the task of stocking and distributing candy as a commercial enterprise in a new movie theater. It is the job of each of the teams to problem-solve and come up with a method for their decision as to which candies to use for their business enterprise. The manner in which they arrive at their stock choices as well as the way in which they defend these choices is what makes up the challenge for this project unit. Metacognitive opportunities are included in the unit to encourage self-reflection (see figures 8.8 and 8.9).

This unit uses recommendations suggested by Caine and Caine (1994) in much the same way as Unit 2 (see pages 113–115).

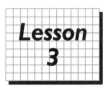

Lesson 3 | Candy Counter Mathematics

Objectives

1. To gain first-hand experience with data research and collation.
2. To create simple bar graphs with labeled axes.
3. To develop the skills of cooperation and teamwork.

Materials

Construction paper, graph paper, rulers, pencils, colored pencils, markers

Vocabulary

1. *tally:* a record or a count of people, things, etc.
2. *poll:* a sampling or collection of opinions on a subject
3. *data:* information organized for analysis
4. *collate:* to assemble in proper sequence
5. *survey:* a detailed investigation
6. *axis (*pl. axes*):* a fixed line on a graph, along which distances are measured
7. *bar graph:* a graph that uses parallel bars of different lengths to show comparison

Task

The project problem posed to the class in this lesson is based on the premise that a new triplex movie theater is coming to the neighborhood. As teams, the students are to make their own plans for a candy counter that they will run in the new theater.

Each group must decide what kind of candy their business will stock and how much they will charge for each item. The manner in which this decision is made is up to the group, but they have to be able to explain and to justify their decisions. Some suggestions for ways in which to establish this justification follow:

- They can poll fellow students and then make a bar graph showing which candy is most popular.

- They can survey people who work at candy concessions at movie theaters to research what candy brands sell the most.
- They can spend a Saturday at a local movie theater observing and tallying how much of each type of candy is bought.

Each team needs to use some form of visual data display for their research, such as a graph or chart (see figure 8.7).

Whatever manner of display they do choose for their data, they must use the display (chart, graph, etc.) in the explanation and defense of their decisions and their conclusions.

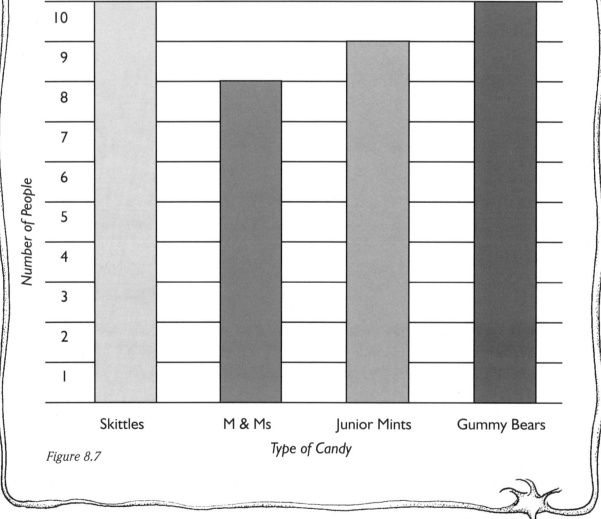

Figure 8.7

PERFORMANCE TASK DATA ASSESSMENT
Elementary Grades

1. Did I make separate columns for each item on my survey?

2. Was my tally done carefully and accurately?

3. Are my numbers in the right order?

4. Do my conclusions make sense?

5. Did I complete all parts of the assignment?

Figure 8.8

SkyLight Training and Publishing, Inc.

PERFORMANCE TASK GRAPH ASSESSMENT
Elementary Grades

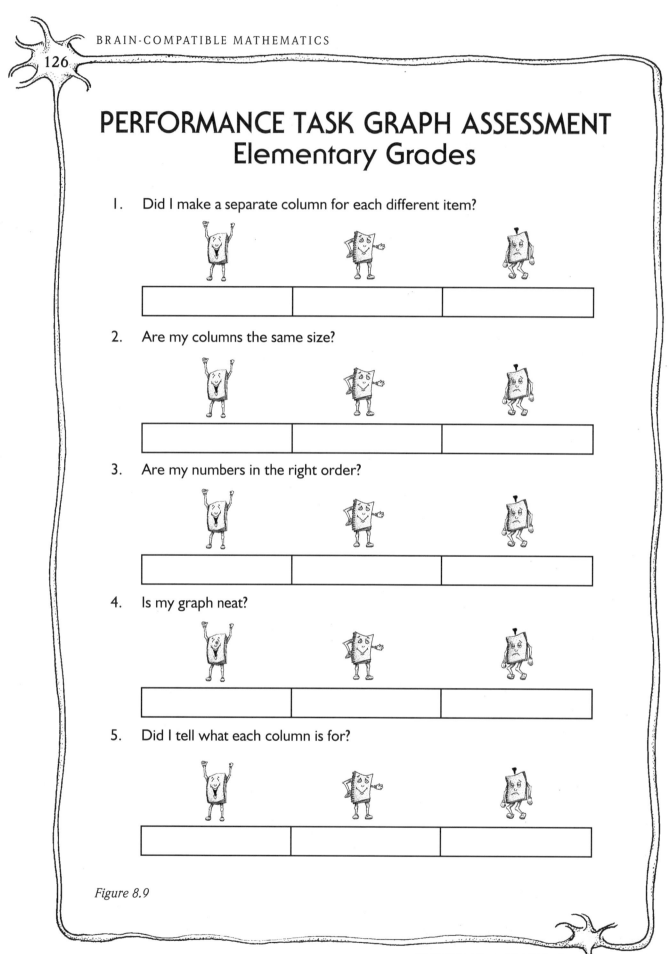

1. Did I make a separate column for each different item?

2. Are my columns the same size?

3. Are my numbers in the right order?

4. Is my graph neat?

5. Did I tell what each column is for?

Figure 8.9

SkyLight Training and Publishing Inc.

ELEMENTARY AND MIDDLE LEVEL TASKS

Chapter 9 address the higher elementary-middle level. (Because it addresses a higher learning level, the unit organization differs slightly from Chapter 8.) The first unit, entitled "Money, Graphs, and All That Jazz!," appeals to linguistic, logical-mathematical, spatial, bodily-kinesthetic, interpersonal, and intrapersonal intelligences. At this level, the linguistic component involves individual reflective writings as well as group discussions. The mathematics has become more sophisticated, and intrapersonal intelligence has been added, being fostered through metacognitive activities such as individual and group reflections. The second unit, entitled "How Do Your Genes Fit?," appeals to a number of intelligences in a similar manner: logical-mathematical, spatial, bodily-kinesthetically, interpersonal, and intrapersonal.

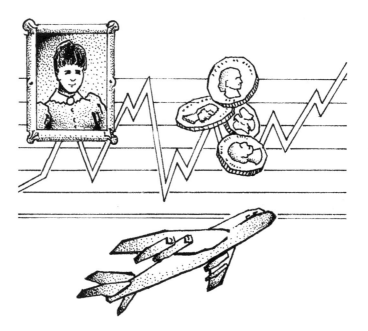

— UNIT ONE —

GRAPHING

Money, Graphs, and All That Jazz!

A popular unit with students, "Money, Graphs, and All That Jazz!" covers interdisciplinary objectives for mathematics, social studies, language arts, and computer science. The main topics studied are data collection, analysis, and representation the way they actually occur in the world outside the classroom. (The Concepts and Vocabulary section is best introduced in language arts class before beginning the mathematics component.)

There are two parts to this unit on graphing. The first part consists of three lessons that showcase bar graphs, circle graphs, and pictographs. This is done through posing problems that require research, data analysis, and the development of inferences and conclusions from that data. The second part, cosisting of lesson 4, showcases line graphs using data from the stock market. The market provides the basis for data research, retrieval, analysis, synthesis, and evaluation.

This unit follows the recommendations of Caine and Caine (1994) for implementation of brain-based learning in schools:

- It provides variety and stimulation.
- The students are creating products and making presentations using their interests as the springboard.
- The cooperative small group (team) model allows for individualized learning plans that are developed according to each student's learning style, assorted intelligences, strengths, interests, and needs.
- The community provides the resources for sample survey populations, ideas for different survey extensions, and stock market information.
- The teacher acts in the capacity of a resource, facilitator, coach, and guide.

The following is a list of Caine and Caine's brain/mind learning principles, as well as the manner in which this unit specifically implements these principles.

1. *The brain is a complex, adaptive system.* Students will adapt and learn in an environment that supports them with cooperative and collaborative group learning, and also challenges them to solve problems that occur in the real world, using data collection and analysis to form their own inferences and conclusions.
2. *The brain is a social brain.* At the middle level, students are especially cognizant of and sensitive to group dynamics. Collaborative and cooperative learning situations are particularly beneficial to the middle-level student; it is at this age that children may be more influenced by peer approval rather than adult approval and become

extremely self-conscious, preferring the safety of a group rather than the danger of appearing to be alone.

3. *The search for meaning is innate.* Students will look for the appearance and relevancy of data in everything around them.

4. *The search for meaning occurs through "patterning."* Through the development of their own surveys or the recording of their stock market data, the students will begin to see how taste patterns and economic patterns occur and repeat throughout the world around them.

5. *Emotions are critical to patterning.* It is important that the learning environment be challenging and exciting for students in this age group or they may lose interest. When interest and excitement are kept at a high level through discussions on such topics as cost of living changes, student surveys, and the stock market, their emotions become linked to the learning, making that learning meaningful, and therefore enduring.

6. *Every brain simultaneously perceives and creates parts and wholes.* Through data collection and collation, the students will experience the individual aspects of statistical research as well as an integrated overview of economics.

7. *Learning involves both focused attention and peripheral perception.* While the students may be focused on their survey or stock market tasks, the teacher's as well as their peer's attitudes towards the lesson become part of the learning experience.

8. *Learning always involves conscious and unconscious processes.* The students may focus on researching their survey or stock data, yet unconsciously, their brains will begin to search out connections between their research and their everyday environment inside and outside the classroom.

9. *We have at least two ways of organizing memory.* Students will find that certain aspects of the lesson become committed to memory so as to allow for instant recall of those experiences when they are needed for future situations having similar characteristics.

10. *Learning is developmental.* Graphing skills and data gathering can be learned at any level of development; however, the more mature the student, the more sophisticated the level of comprehension. This particular unit is most appropriate for middle-level students.

11. *Complex learning is enhanced by challenge and inhibited by threat.* This is the reason why group learning at the middle level is so successful. The students feel safe within the group environment, constructive socialization and communication are encouraged, and a state of "relaxed alertness" can be maintained. A state of relaxed alertness is one in which optimal learning occurs through the maintenance of a physically relaxed nervous system and a sense of security (in teaching terms, a safe, nonthreatening classroom environment that values risk taking and experimentation).

12. *Every brain is uniquely organized*, and as such, will interpret information and lesson directions in an individual manner.

The contextual learning is designed around student interests. All of the team learning is structured around genuine issues and problems. The learning takes place outside the classroom as well as inside. Students have the opportunity to monitor their own learning and maximize that learning through metacognitive as well as group and self-evaluation activities.

Interdisciplinary Objectives

Statistics has emerged as a major component of the school mathematics curriculum during the 1990s (NCTM 1989). We know that understanding the statistical investigation process is central to working with statistics. A statistical investigation typically involves four components: (1) posing the question, (2) collecting data, (3) analyzing data, and (4) interpreting the results. In this unit, students will also include a fifth component, that of communicating their results.

Although a central goal is to understand how students use the process of statistical investigation within the broader context of problem solving, it is also important to look at a student's understanding as related to concepts linked to this process. In other words, what it means to understand and use graphs is central to what is involved in knowing and being able to do statistics. Typically, students are asked only to read information from graphs. However, we may need to rethink not only the nature of graphs, but also questions about using and reading graphs so as to help students better understand their uses.

General Objectives

1. To experience, through self-evaluation and self-reflection, the difference between low and high lesson expectations for oneself, as well as one's peers.
2. To further develop organizational as well as self-reliance skills.
3. To develop and refine collaborative group skills such as positive interdependence, communication, conflict resolution, and teamwork.

Math Objectives

1. To experience gathering and collating data.
2. To identify and work with different types of graphs.
3. To increase student awareness of finances and today's cost of living.
4. To understand concepts such as interest, inflation, mean, median, and mode.
5. To reinforce estimation skills using decimals and fractions as well as percents.
6. To review correct procedures for the employment of fractions, decimals, and percents.
7. To develop an understanding of basic financial and statistical terminology.

Computer Science Objectives

1. To use a computer graphing program.
2. To refine word processing skills.

Social Studies Objectives

1. To better understand global economic factors and their influence on the United States, through the study of the stock market.
2. To understand the concepts of supply and demand.

Language Arts Objectives

1. To learn and use economic, mathematic, and computer science vocabulary.
2. To employ such vocabulary in written reflections and evaluations.

Foreign Language Objectives

1. To learn the basic vocabulary in a foreign language for numbers and simple computation terminology.
2. To use and be able to follow simple calculator directions in a foreign language, as well as give the correct mathematical answers in that language.

Concepts and Vocabulary

The following list of basic graphing, finance, and economic terms is designed to encourage the students to express their thoughts using both oral and written methods. Good communication skills require an adequate working vocabulary for clear explanations as well as thought-provoking reflections.

This vocabulary is first introduced in language arts class, where instruction is carried out through visual demonstration whenever possible to engage visual as well as aural learners.

Opportunities for math class and group discussions as well as individual verbalizations should be carried out prior to any and all written mathematic work. Such discussions allow for the extra processing time needed for assimilation of new information. Repeated use of financing and graphing terminology in correct context results in greater student comfort level, which further translates into higher quality written and reflective work.

1. *collate:* to assemble in proper sequence
2. *data:* information organized for analysis
3. *survey:* a detailed investigation
4. *inflation:* an abnormal increase in money, resulting in rising prices
5. *deflation:* a reduction in value or amount of money resulting in decreased prices
6. *depression:* a period of drastic decline in the national economy
7. *recession:* a moderate, temporary decline in economic activity
8. *trend:* the particular direction in which things go, or change course
9. *axis (pl. axes):* a fixed line along which distances are measured
10. *distribution:* how the data spreads out in a graph
11. *frequency:* the number of times the same thing occurs in a set of data
12. *line graph:* a network of lines connecting different points, each of which represents a value or number

13. *bar graph:* a graph that uses parallel bars of different lengths to show a comparison

14. *circle graph:* a pie graph usually used to show percentages

15. *pictograph:* a graph with symbolic figures, each representing a certain number of people, cars, etc.

16. *range:* the difference between the highest and the lowest numbers in a set of data

17. *mean:* the average of a set of numbers

18. *median:* the middle number in a set of ordered numbers

19. *mode:* the number which appears most often in a set of numbers

20. *rubric:* a plan or framework for how work will be evaluated

21. *expenditure:* the act of spending

22. *interest:* an amount charged for borrowing money, or the amount paid on invested money

23. *principal:* the original amount of money a depositor places in a savings account; or the original amount of money borrowed for a loan

24. *capital:* any moneys used for carrying on business

25. *dividend:* profit (money or stock) paid to a shareholder

26. *earnings:* money made on investments

27. *spreadsheet:* a worksheet showing related items side by side in parallel columns

28. *stock:* the capital which a corporation makes through the sale of its shares

29. *profits:* money made from investments after all expenses have been met

30. *shares:* any of the equal parts into which the capital stock of the company is divided

Introduction to Lessons

The first three lessons deal with bar graphs, circle graphs, and pictographs. Before introducing these lessons, read lesson 4, "The Stock Market: Ways to Make Your Money Work for You!" This particular aspect of the data gathering must be initiated prior to any other work, as this component involves collecting stock market quotes over a four-week period.

LESSON 1: What Do You Cost?

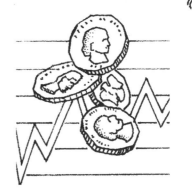

Lesson 1 begins with the assignment of Project Sheet 1 (see figure 9.1) as homework the night before the first lesson. By beginning with an assignment, an anticipatory set is established, and the data that is needed for the first class (student findings as to the varying cost of those items listed on the project sheet) is readily available. A tally for each of the items listed is drawn on the classroom chalkboard.

The class follows the directions for the graph construction as described in lesson 1. The class computes the average dollar amount spent for each of the listed items, keeping separate averages, one for girls and another for boys. The students are then grouped in pairs so as to provide each other with support and communication during the graph construction. The teacher uses student samples of previous work to illustrate the different benchmark levels on the rubric scale before the students begin their graph constructions. See chapter 6 for the benchmark rubric indicating which of the samples are at each of the four levels: novice, basic, proficient, or advanced (figure 6.1). The characteristics that make up a good bar graph are then discussed by the entire class, after which the students begin to work with their partners, discussing their ideas and questions, each individual creating his or her own graph (see figure 9.2). The teacher circulates throughout the room, acting as a guide/coach, always available for help in case the students have questions or problems.

When the graphs are completed, the class evaluation takes place amid a display of all the graphs (much like an exhibit or an expo). Each student is responsible for writing an Individual Evaluation (see figure 9.3). A class discussion follows as to which of the graphs are the strongest and why, as well as which are in need of improvement and what kind of improvements might be best.

PROJECT SHEET 1
What Do You Cost?

Name:_____ Section:_____ Date:_____

Do you know how expensive you are? With your parents' help, find out how much you really cost. Listed below are some "think about it" statements to get you started.

1. I spent _____ on my newest pair of sneakers.

2. I spend _____ on lunch and snacks every week.

3. I spent _____ on the last movie ticket I bought.

4. It cost _____ for the activity fee, equipment, supplies, and/or uniform for my latest sport or hobby.

5. I spent _____ on my newest pair of jeans.

6. My last haircut cost _____ .

7. My last doctor's visit cost _____ .

8. I spent _____ the last time I bought a tape/CD.

9. I spent _____ on the last present I bought for someone.

10. I spent _____ so far this year on school supplies.

This is only a partial list of how much you cost. Survey your family and on the bottom of this page list some other expenditures they have to make on your behalf.

Figure 9.1

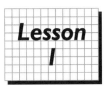

Lesson 1

What Do You Cost?: Food, Clothing, Shelter, Etc.

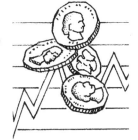

Objective

To increase student awareness of the cost of raising a child today.

Skills

- Conducting a family survey.
- Presenting data visually.
- Using survey and graph data to draw conclusions.

Class Discussion

- What did you learn about the amount of money spent on you?
- Why was the title "What Do You Cost?" an appropriate one?
- What dollar amount on the survey most surprised you?
- How did this survey help you to better understand the cost of raising a child today?

Task

Have the class find the average (mean) dollar amount spent on both boys and girls for the items listed. Each student is to construct his or her own bar graph representing the collated data for both girls and boys. All bar graphs will be displayed for the class evaluation. Emphasis of bar graph qualities should include the following:

- Bars must be of equal size.
- Bars must be evenly spaced.
- Graph must be easy to read.
- Graph must have a title.
- The graph must have a key if appropriate.

The class bar graph evaluation is designed to help the students organize their thoughts in writing, and should be carried out only after the class discussion has been completed.

WHAT DO YOU COST?

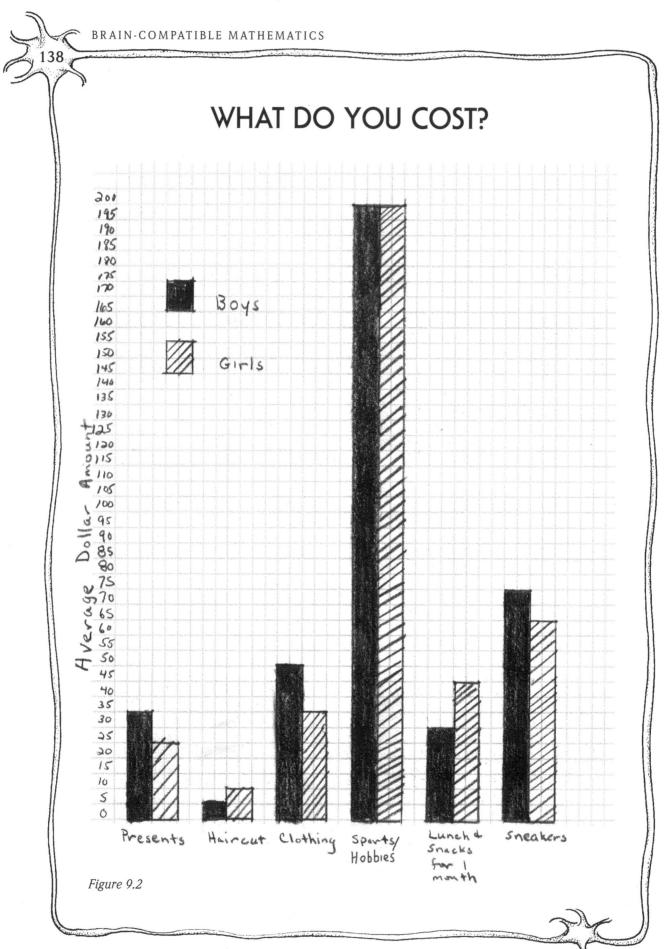

Figure 9.2

INDIVIDUAL EVALUATION
Class Bar Graphs

Name:_____ Section:_____ Date:_____

I think graph #____ is the best graph. My reasons for choosing this graph are:

    1.

    2.

    3.

I think the graph would have been better if the person had:

    1.

    2.

I think graph # ____ is the weakest graph. The reasons I think this graph needs more work are:

    1.

    2.

    3.

If this had been my graph, I would have:

Figure 9.3

LESSON 2: Yesterday–Today: How Prices Have Changed!

Lesson 2 involves the creation of a triple bar graph for which the students gather their data much in the same manner as the previous lesson. This time, however, they must research for three different sets of data: one for item prices in the 1950s, another for the 1980s, and one for the cost of those same items today (see figure 9.4 for an example of this type of graph using different dates). This data-gathering assignment is presented in Project Sheet 2 (see figure 9.5).

THEN AND NOW

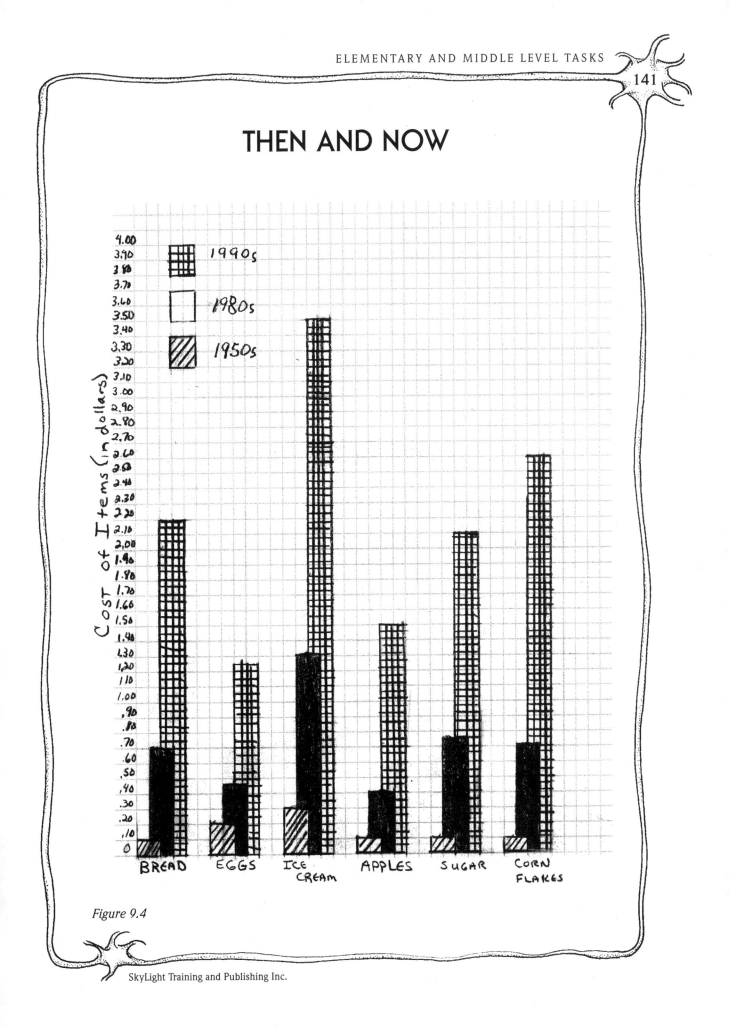

Figure 9.4

PROJECT SHEET 2

Yesterday–Today: How Prices Have Changed!

Name:_____ Section:_____ Date:_____

Fill in the chart below to see how prices have changed over the years. Visit stores, read newspaper advertisements, or look in your own kitchen to see what has happened to prices since the 1950s.

Item	1950s	1980s	Today
Bread (1 lb.)	$0.10	_____	_____
Eggs (1 doz.)	$0.20	_____	_____
Ice Cream ($^1/_2$ gal.)	$0.30	_____	_____
Apples (1 lb.)	$0.10	_____	_____
Sugar (5 lbs.)	$0.10	_____	_____
Corn Flakes (16 oz.)	$0.10	_____	_____

Ask older friends and family to help. How much did each of the items above, as well as the items below, cost when your family members were younger? What do they cost today?

Bicycle _____   Candy Bar _____   Car _____

1 Gallon Gasoline _____   Movie Ticket _____   Pair of Shoes _____

We will be collating this data for a new bar graph in our next class.

Figure 9.5

SkyLight Training and Publishing Inc.

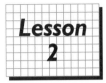

Yesterday–Today: How Prices Have Changed!

Lesson 2

Objectives
- To understand the concepts of supply, demand, and inflation.
- To provide "hands-on" practice in graph construction.

Skills
- Researching specific information.
- Understanding the relationship between value and cost.
- Comprehending how cost changes with supply and demand as well as inflation.
- Correctly setting up a graph and the label axes.

Class Discussion
- What did you learn about the direction prices have taken since 1950?
- Do prices always increase? If so, why? If not, why?
- Does this pattern always hold true?
- Why do stores run seasonal sales?
- What was "The Great Depression"?
- What happened to the cost of things during that time?
- What might be some of the reasons for inflation?
- What might be some reasons for deflation?

Task 1
Using the information from three generations of prices (1950, 1980, and today), construct a bar graph to display this information in a clear and easily understood manner.

Task 2
Using the same data as in Task 1, construct at least one bar graph on the computer using a computer graphing program.

LESSON 3: Which Graph Works Best?
Comparing and Contrasting
Different Kinds of Graphs

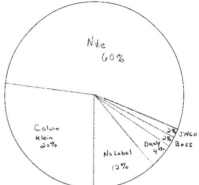

Lesson 3 involves the comparison of different kinds of graphs. Before beginning this comparison, a review of circle graph construction is recommended, using Constructing a Circle Graph: An Introduction to Lesson 3 (see figure 9.6). Using the model Circle Graph (see figure 9.7) for the individual survey project assignment, students are given the choice of surveying topics that interest them, or using the lesson outline suggestion of ice cream flavors (each class chooses its own survey topic). See figure 9.8 for a student-made example of a circle graph for this project.

The group graph project ("Which Graph Works Best?") is explained in detail below. This project involves the students working together in teams of three or four. Each team chooses their own research topic for the survey, enabling them to experience the sense of project ownership. For help in organizing and presenting this unit, see Project Sheet 3 (figure 9.9) and the Problem Ladder Graphic Organizer (figure 9.10).

The seventh grade uses sixth grade students as their database, the sixth grade uses fifth grade students as a database, and so on. Having the students always survey the previous grade creates a feeling of continuity since the database students become the following year's survey takers. In this manner, they are primed and excited about doing the project before it has even been introduced.

The students enjoy the idea of traveling with their teams and visiting each of the database grade classes to gather their information. The younger students are flattered that the older students are paying attention to them, and the groundwork has been laid for a positive inter-grade experience. It is recommended, however, that a letter to the database grade teachers be circulated the week prior to starting the project. The letter should inform those teachers of your plans, give them an idea as to when the student visits will take place, and allow for the communication of possible conflicts.

When all the graphs have been completed, each team presents its findings to the entire class, using their graphs to illustrate their conclusions. The students then evaluate each other, using the forms suggested by figures 9.11 and 9.12. Finally the students evaluate their own projects, using the self-assessment provided in figure 9.13. These metacognitive self-assessments offer the students an opportunity to reflect upon their new learning, and process how they might have use for either the new knowledge or what they have learned about data and statistics while in the process of acquiring this knowledge.

CONSTRUCTING A CIRCLE GRAPH
An Introduction to Lesson 3

Name:_____ Section:_____ Date:_____

A circle graph (pie graph) is a graph that shows how information is segmented according to percentages. In other words, one quarter of your circle is equal to 25% of your sample data.

An easy way to design a circle graph is to divide the circle into 10 equal sections, each of the sections representing 10% of the total circle. You can do this by drawing a diameter that cuts the circle into 2 equal halves. Once you find the circle's center, place your protractor on the vertex, using the diameter as a straight angle. You then measure 5 congruent acute angles, each one 36°.

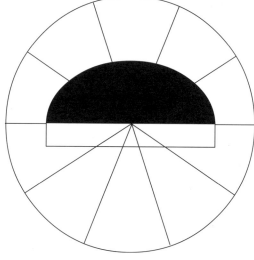

Draw the lines of the angle through the vertex, so as to divide the other half of the circle into an additional 5 congruent segments.

How many total congruent sections do you have now? _____ If the entire circle is 100%, what is the percentage value of each of these sections? _____

Assignment

Using the 5 choices of ice cream flavors selected by the class, interview 50 people to find which one of the choices is their favorite. Construct a circle graph using the method we just learned in class. (If there are 50 people surveyed, what is the percentage value of each person?)

Figure 9.6

SkyLight Training and Publishing Inc.

CIRCLE GRAPH

Name:_____ Section:_____ Date:_____

Figure 9.7

FAVORITE CLOTHING LABELS
OF 7TH GRADERS
Circle Graph

Name:_____ Date:_____

Section: _____

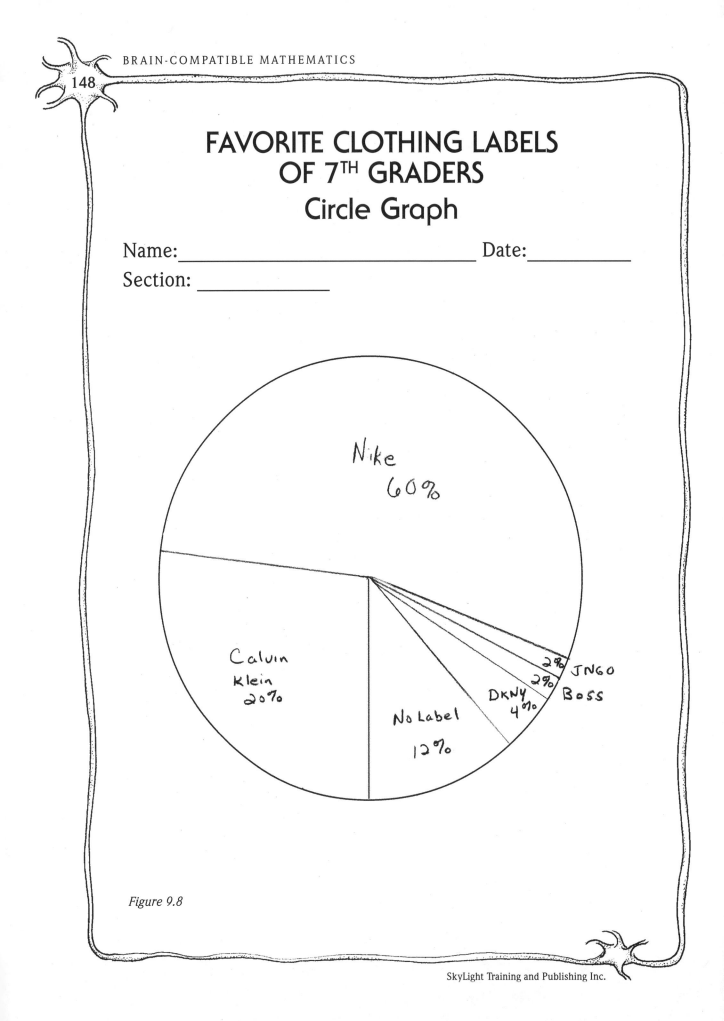

Nike
60%

Calvin
Klein
20%

No Label
12%

DKNY
4%

2% JNGO

2% BOSS

Figure 9.8

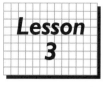

Lesson 3

Which Graph Works Best? Comparing and Contrasting Different Kinds of Graphs

Objective

To identify and work with different kinds of graphs.

Skills

- Collating original data and constructing three different types of graphs for the same data.
- Comparing and contrasting the readability, strengths, and weaknesses of each graph type for that same data.

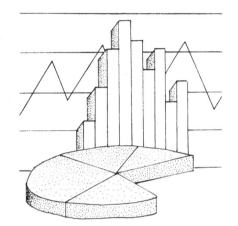

Class Discussion

See Project Sheet 3 (figure 9.9).

Task

Students will work in groups (teams) of three or four. Each team will choose an original topic for a survey of the sixth grade (see Project Sheet 3). The teams will then gather data from their sample population (the sixth grade students), collate their data, and construct three graphs as a team: a bar graph, a circle graph, and a pictograph, each using the identical set of data. Each team will submit a written report describing the organization of their study, their data-gathering methods, and their conclusions. The teams will then present their findings to the class in an oral report using visual supports (graphs). The final oral presentation will also include an evaluation of the different graph types, listing positive and negative aspects as well as the appropriateness of each graph type in regard to the data.

Conclusion

The groups will present their surveys and graphs to the class. The class will then evaluate these presentations (see figures 9.11 and 9.12).

PROJECT SHEET 3
Comparing and Contrasting Graphs

Name: _____   Section:_____   Date: _____

Discussion Questions

What kind of graph is pictured in this cartoon?

"That's the last trip I'll take for some R & R!"

- What do the vertical and horizontal axes represent?
- What happened when the character took his trip for rest and relaxation?
  (What could have happened when he was away to cause this result?)

Graph Types

- A *line graph* with time as the horizontal axis shows a trend. Data appropriate for a line graph are temperature, price, population, etc.
- A *bar graph* shows differences by using different sizes of rectangular bars to represent the different amounts.
- A *circle graph* using percent shows visually how all the information can be divided to display the distribution of the data.
- A *pictograph* displays data in an organized and easily visualized manner using pictures to represent the distribution of the data.

Project Directions

Your team will survey a sample of 100 sixth-grade students on an original topic. Collate and develop your team's results as bar graphs, circle graphs, and pictographs. Each team will be evaluated by your classmates as to

- the accuracy of the graphs,
- the readability of the graphs,
- the originality and creativity of the graphs, and
- the way in which the data were organized and displayed. (Was it eye-catching? Did it give the viewer a visual understanding of the data at a glance?)

Figure 9.9

PROBLEM LADDER GRAPHIC ORGANIZER

Curriculum Area(s): *Mathematics: data collation & graphing* Project Length: *4 weeks*

Performance Task Title: *Sixth Grade Survey* Grade Level(s): *5–8*

Resources/Materials: *Poster board, markers, rulers, compass, protractor, construction paper, glue*

TASK DESCRIPTION

Students will work in groups (teams) of three or four. Each team will choose an original topic for use in a survey. The teams will then gather data from their sample population, collate their data, and construct three graphs as a team: a bar graph, a circle graph, and a pictograph, each using the identical set of data. Each team will submit a written report describing the organization of their study, their data-gathering methods, and their conclusions. The teams will then present their findings to the class in an oral report using visual supports (graphs). The final oral presentation will also include an evaluation of the different graph types, listing positive and negative aspects as well as the appropriateness of each graph type in regard to the data.

PROJECT OBJECTIVES

Student comprehension of concepts

- *identifying and working with different graphs*
- *gathering and collating data*
- *organizing a survey and communicating results*

Student skill and process development

- *estimation*
- *fractions, decimals, and percent*
- *technology*

PRODUCTS AND/OR PERFORMANCES

Written Report

describes: (1) survey organization, (2) data gathering and collation procedures, and (3) conclusions

Graph Displays

circle graph, bar graph, and pictograph for identical sets of data

Oral Report

describes survey organization, data gathering and collation procedures, and conclusions

CRITERIA FOR PRODUCT EVALUATION

Group Products

- *information was clear and easy to understand*
- *complete sentences and correct spelling were used throughout*
- *all 3 required parts were included*

Individual Products

- *equal increments on axes*
- *bars of uniform size*
- *accurate representation of data*
- *appropriate title*
- *key, if appropriate*

Extensions

- *information was clear and easy to understand*
- *voices well modulated with clear enunciation*
- *all members presented*

Figure 9.10

INDIVIDUAL SURVEYS
Graph Evaluations

Name: _____ Section: _____ Date: _____

Each of the following categories will be given a value of 1 to 4, 1 being the lowest grade and 4 being the highest.

Group Members: _____

_____ 1. Data were accurate, valid, and well-organized.

_____ 2. Axes were labeled correctly.

_____ 3. Graph was accurate, comprehensive, well-drawn, and easy to understand.

_____ 4. Graph could be easily read and understood from a distance.

_____ 5. Choice of graph type (line graph, bar graph, circle graph, etc.) was appropriate for the information being displayed.

_____ 6. Graph was presented in an original, unique and creative manner.

_____   TOTAL POINTS

In a paragraph, explain why you gave the graph this grade. What did you like most about this graph? What did you like least? If this were your graph, how would you have made it better? _____

_____
_____
_____
_____
_____
_____
_____
_____
_____

Figure 9.11

SkyLight Training and Publishing Inc.

GRAPH SURVEYS
Evaluation of Group Presentation

Name:_____ Section:_____ Date:_____

Group Members:_____

Each of the following categories will be awarded a grade of 1 to 4,
4 representing "excellent" and 1 representing "poor."

_____ 1. The presentation was accurate, comprehensive, organized, informative, and easy to understand.

_____ 2. All the graphs and charts were easy to read, understand, and contained valid, accurate information.

_____ 3. The presentation had a clear beginning, middle, and end.

_____ 4. *Everyone* on the team was well prepared and made valuable contributions to the presentation.

_____ TOTAL POINTS

Explain below why you gave this grade. Be sure to use complete sentences in your paragraph.

1. The part of this presentation that I liked best was_____

_____

2. The reason I liked this part of the presentation best was_____

_____

3. If this were my presentation, I would change_____

_____

4. I would do this part differently because_____

_____

5. I thought this group worked well together (poorly together) because_____

_____

6. I thought this presentation was interesting (boring) because_____

_____

7. I think it would have been a better presentation if _____

_____

Figure 9.12

SkyLight Training and Publishing Inc.

SURVEY GRAPH PROJECT
Standards for Self-Grading (page 1)

Student self-grading outline for the graphing project.

Name:_____ Section:_____ Date:_____

How to Grade Your Report
- Report Content and Mathematical Accuracy: Were all the questions answered completely and correctly? 65%
- Writing Skills: Was the report well written? (Did it have correct spelling and sentence structure?) 25%
- Appearance: Was the report neat and well organized? 10%

In addition to the above numerical grade, you are to give yourself an effort grade as described below:

How to Grade Your Effort
The effort grade may be calculated by counting each *(E)* as 25 points, each *(S)* as 15 points, and each *(U)* as 5 points. (For example if there are 2 *(E)*s and 2 *(S)*s, the grade will be 80%.)

SUPERIOR: (E)
___ My work was superior/excellent.
___ I made many positive contributions to the group effort in every way possible.
___ I encouraged other members and assisted them whenever they needed help.
___ I was key to my group's success.

SATISFACTORY: (S)
___ My work was complete and correct.
___ I made several positive contributions to the group effort.
___ I encouraged at least one group member.
___ I helped my group succeed.

Figure 9.13a

SURVEY GRAPH PROJECT
Standards for Self-Grading (page 2)

UNSATISFACTORY: (U)

___ I could have done better.

___ I did not encourage others.

___ I did not worry about my group.

___ I kind of goofed off.

Reflection

1. What did you learn about graphs from this project that you didn't know before?

2. Did you find any part of this project difficult? If so, which part?

3. Was there any part of the project which you liked best? Why did you like that part?

4. What did you enjoy or not enjoy about working with your team members?

5. Do you prefer to work in groups of two, three, or four? Why?

6. How do you feel about our math class right now?

7. What do you think we can we do to improve our math class?

On the back of this sheet, explain in four or five complete sentences the reasons for the grade you gave. Which of your team members were most helpful? Which were least helpful? How were they or weren't they helpful?

Figure 9.13b

LESSON 4: The Stock Market

The second part of this unit, the stock market segment, examines line graphs in detail. The project is explained in lesson 4, "Ways to Make Your Money Work for You!" In this project the students are each given a theoretical $500 to invest. Working in pairs, they have twice the investment they would have had as individuals. The teacher keeps an ongoing spreadsheet of stock quotes for a three-week period (which is why this part of the unit is introduced before lesson 1 even begins).

Each day the students copy their stocks' closing prices from the previous day. A large version of the spreadsheet is posted at the side of the room for the entire run of the unit. This spreadsheet serves as a reference guide to prevent unnecessary errors and so that blank spaces on the students' spreadsheets can be checked and/or corrected. At the end of the three-week period, after the student survey has been completed, most of the necessary data for this part of the unit has already been collected. (The final week's stock quotes are added during the time the students are working on the stock graph.) Following are complete project directions, as well as outlines for evaluation and metacognitive reflection.

Lesson 4

The Stock Market: Ways to Make Your Money Work for You!

Objectives

- To familiarize students with basic investment terminology and ideas.
- To gain hands-on experience constructing complex line graphs.

Skills

- Developing an awareness of investment alternatives.
- Developing an awareness of economic trends and cycles.
- Developing a more sophisticated sense of the line graph's function.

Class Discussion

Just as a bank pays dividends to its investors, a company or corporation pays dividends to its investors (people who buy a share in the company). There are many different ways to invest money. Some ways involve more risk than others.

- The purchase of stock shares is an example of an investment.
  - Do you or does someone in your family own shares of stock?
  - Do you know how shares are acquired?
  - Who gets the money when you buy a share of stock?
  - What do you think the company does with this money?
  - What does the company give you for your money?
- Why might people who run a company sell shares in the company?
- In this context, what is the meaning of the word "risk"?
- Why are some investments riskier than others?
- Why might a "high-risk" investment pay more than one posing less risk?

Task

Students are each given a theoretical $500 to invest. They then pair up, "pool" their money, and select 6 to 7 stocks from a previously selected group of 20 choices. These stocks are to be tracked over a 4-week period on a spreadsheet as well as a daily line graph (one graph per stock).

At the end of the 4-week period, students will combine the separate graphs into one long "multi-graph" by cutting and taping so as to have one continuous graph displaying the team's total stock data. The difficulties that the students may have to deal with such as overlapping data, or even multiple overlaps, will provide a complex yet not unmanageable challenge so long as in the final version each stock's line graph is color coded.

For the final graph, the teams will rule up three 12"x18" sheets of paper that are attached horizontally at the top and bottom of the page, and upon which the final graph is to be plotted and displayed. While the axes and range of data were mapped out on the practice multi-graph, the final version will take the data directly from the spreadsheets so as to reduce the possibility of error due to carelessness.

Students as well as the teacher will assess the final graphs as to their accuracy, readability, neatness, and ease of comprehension (see figures 9.14-9.16).

STUDENT STOCK GRAPH
Exhibit Evaluation

Name: _____ Section:_____ Date:_____

From all the displayed graphs, choose the one you like best. In a complete paragraph, explain why you chose this graph.

Next, choose the graph that you think needs the most improvement. Give your reasons for this choice as well.

You may wish to use the following questions as a guide for your paragraph.

1. Was the information in the graph accurate? Was it valid?

2. Was the graph easy to read and understand? What was it about the graph that made it easy to understand, or what made the graph confusing?

3. Did the graph make it clear as to which of the stocks was the better investment? What was it about the graph that made this clear or made it confusing? What could be done to make this information easier to understand?

4. If this were your graph, would you do anything to improve it? If so, what would you do? _____

_____

_____

_____

_____

_____

_____

_____

_____

_____

_____

_____

Figure 9.14

SkyLight Training and Publishing Inc.

TEAM INVESTMENT PRESENTATION
Evaluation of Group Presentation

Outline for Evaluation Paragraph

Refer to Rubric for Group Project Presentations (see chapter 6).
Each team will have the opportunity to present the results of their stock market "investments." These teams will be evaluated on the basis of their data presentations as follows:

1. Was the team graph accurate, easy to read, and easy to understand?
    What was it about the graph that made it easy or difficult to understand?

2. Was it clear as to which of the stocks was the better investment?
    What was it about the graph that made this clear or unclear?
    If the information was confusing, what could be done to improve the clarity of the results?

3. Was it clear that the group worked as a team, or did it appear as if only one of the students did most of the work?
    What was it about the presentation that gave you this impression?

4. In a few sentences, explain what you thought was the strongest part of this team's presentation.
    What was the weakest part?
    What do you think would have improved this presentation?

Figure 9.15

SURVEY GRAPH PROJECT
Standards for Self-Grading (page 1)

Student self-grading outline for the stock market project.

Name:_____ Section:_____ Date:_____

How to Grade Your Report
- Report Content and Mathematical Accuracy: Were all the questions answered completely and correctly? 65%
- Writing Skills: Was the report well written? (Did it have correct spelling and sentence structure?) 25%
- Appearance: Was the report neat and well organized? 10%

In addition to the above numerical grade, you are to give yourself an effort grade as described below:

How to Grade Your Effort
The effort grade may be calculated by counting each *(E)* as 25 points, each *(S)* as 15 points, and each *(U)* as 5 points. (For example if there are 2 *(E)*s and 2 *(S)*s, the grade will be 80%.)

SUPERIOR: (E)
___ My work was superior/excellent.
___ I made many positive contributions to the group effort in every way possible.
___ I encouraged other members and assisted them whenever they needed help.
___ I was key to my group's success.

SATISFACTORY: (S)
___ My work was complete and correct.
___ I made several positive contributions to the group effort.
___ I encouraged at least one group member.
___ I helped my group succeed.

Figure 9.16a

SURVEY GRAPH PROJECT
Standards for Self-Grading (page 2)

UNSATISFACTORY: (U)

___ I could have done better.

___ I did not encourage others.

___ I did not worry about my group.

___ I kind of goofed off.

Reflections

1. What did you learn about graphs from this project that you didn't know before?

2. Did you find any part of this project difficult? If so, which part?

3. Was there any part of the project which you liked best? Why did you like that part?

4. What did you enjoy or not enjoy about working with your team members?

5. Do you prefer to work in groups of two, three, or four? Why?

6. How do you feel about our math class right now?

7. What do you think we can we do to improve our math class?

On the back of this sheet, explain in four or five complete sentences the reasons for the grade you gave. Which of your team members were most helpful? Which were least helpful? How were they or weren't they helpful?

Figure 9.16b

— UNIT TWO —

PROBABILITY AND GENETICS

How Do Your Genes Fit?

In this unit, interdisciplinary objectives for both mathematics and science are covered. The Probability and Genetics Vocabulary words are best introduced in language arts class prior to beginning either the mathematics or science component.

The introductory mathematics component (see lesson 1) consists of two probability tasks designed to help the students become familiar with those concepts involved with probability work.

The overview for the actual combined mathematics/science project component (see lesson 2).

This unit, just as the previous one, uses Caine and Caine's recommendations for the implementation of brain-based learning in schools.

- It provides variety and stimulation.
- The students are creating products and making presentations using their interests as the springboard.
- The group (team) model allows for individualized learning plans that are developed according to each student's learning style, assorted intelligences, strengths, interests, and needs.
- The community provides the resources for sample survey populations and ideas for different survey extensions.
- The teacher acts in the capacity of a resource, facilitator, coach, and guide.

The following is a list of Caine and Caine's brain/mind learning principles, as well as the manner in which this unit specifically implements these principles.

1. *The brain is a complex, adaptive system.* Students will adapt and learn in an environment that supports them by encouraging teamwork while challenging them to learn interdisciplinary concepts in both mathematics and science.

2. *The brain is a social brain.* For this reason, the interpersonal strengths of each student are developed and expanded through the cooperative and collaborative group learning format.

3. *The search for meaning is innate.* Students will find meaning and relevancy in this task since genetics and families are a large part of their present and their future lives.

4. *The search for meaning occurs through "patterning,"* and it is through the investigation of the science of genetics that students can observe first-hand how examples of patterning occur within the human body itself.

5. *Emotions are critical to patterning.* It is important that the learning environment be challenging, exciting, and nonthreatening. The ego-centric involvement with genetics in relation to students' present and future lives involves each student emotionally. Their curiosity will provide intrinsic motivation, and the nonthreatening collaborative environment makes this learning experience brain-compatible.

6. *Every brain simultaneously perceives and creates parts and wholes.* Students will perceive the personal aspects of this activity, at the same time comprehending its implications for all of humankind.

7. *Learning involves both focused attention and peripheral perception.* While each student may be focused on his or her task, the teacher's attitude and enthusiasm as well as other students' attitudes towards the project become an integral part of the learning experience.

8. *Learning always involves conscious and unconscious processes.* The students may focus on specific aspects of the activity, yet on a subconscious level their brains will search for connections to similar applications.

9. *We have at least two ways of organizing memory.* We have a set of systems for receiving relatively unrelated information. There is a part of our brains geared to rote memorization, as well as a spatial/autobiographical memory that does not need rehearsal, and which allows for instant recall of experiences. This project has such a high level of appeal to a young adolescent that it will be stored as autobiographical memory.

10. *Learning is developmental.* Probability can be learned at any level of development. This unit is appropriate for upper elementary and middle levels.

11. *Complex learning is enhanced by challenge and inhibited by threat.* It is for this reason that learning experiences be nonthreatening, relevant, and enjoyable.

12. *Every brain is uniquely organized,* and as such, will interpret information and project directions in an individual manner, thereby encouraging the learner to become increasingly self-confident, self-reliant, and self-sufficient.

The contextual learning is designed around student interests. All of the learning is structured around real issues and problems. The students work together in teams. The learning takes place outside the classroom as well as inside. Students have the opportunity to monitor their own learning as well as maximize that learning. Metacognitive opportunities are also included in the unit to encourage self-reflection.

Because parental support is necessary in supplying family history information, this unit begins with a letter to parents stating its goals and benefits (see figure 9.17).

Dear Parents:

Our math and science students will shortly begin a unit on probability and genetics. Probability has an impact upon our everyday lives. An intuitive understanding of probability as well as the ability to analyze data are vital skills for success in today's world.

The goal of this unit, in addition to being an extension of the science unit on reproduction, is to give the students a hands-on experience in choosing appropriate strategies for problem solving. The students will find themselves drawing from past knowledge and experience as they progress in a logical and sequential manner toward their conclusions. They will begin to develop the critical thinking skills so vital today, skills necessary to create multiple strategies for multiple solutions.

We appreciate the support and encouragement you have shown in the past, and once again invite you to join in the project with us.

Sincerely,

Math Teacher
Science Teacher

Figure 9.17

Math and Science Objectives

1. Students will gain hands-on experience with the collection, organization, and assessment of data.
2. Students will gain first-hand experience with the use of elementary probability models and the application of those models to genetic outcomes.
3. Students will learn to use the scientific method as a tool to aid in the analysis of data and probability predictions.
4. Students will continue the development of their critical thinking skills, as well as learn to evaluate conclusions drawn by others.
5. Students will learn to draw correlations, both positive and negative, from data gathered.
6. Students will gain the knowledge as to how the science of genetics works via the application of the scientific method.
7. Students will develop vocabulary pertinent to this unit.
8. Students will learn peer and self-evaluation skills.
9. Students will learn positive group dynamics and a team approach to problem solving.

Vocabulary

1. *data:* facts, information, or statistics arrived at through calculations or experimentation
2. *data analysis:* an investigation based on collected facts, information, or statistics
3. *correlation:* a mutual relationship of two or more things
4. *positive correlation:* a mutual relationship of two things that change in the same direction (an increase in one results in an increase in the other)
5. *negative correlation:* a mutual relationship of two things that change in opposite directions (an increase in one results in a decrease in the other)
6. *zero correlation:* a relationship of two things where change in one does not correspond to any change in the other
7. *probability:* the relative possibility that an event will happen

8. *probability model:* a formula, table, or a chart used to make predictions of events that will happen in the future

9. *predictable outcomes:* results that can be figured out in advance

10. *gene:* the unit that controls the development of the characteristics we inherit from our natural parents

11. *chromosome:* thread-like material in the cell nucleus that carries the hereditary material (inherited characteristics)

12. *dominant genes:* hereditary material that most often results in observable physical characteristics

13. *recessive genes:* hereditary material that is present, but might not result in a physical characteristic (it can, however, be passed on to future generations)

14. *mutant genes:* hereditary material that has been changed from its original form

15. *deoxyribonucleic acid (DNA):* material found in the cell nucleus that functions in the transference of inherited (genetic) characteristics

16. *inherited characteristics:* attributes passed from biological parents to their children

17. *offspring:* biological children

18. *sibling:* a brother or a sister

19. *hereditary history:* the record of genetic characteristics passed from biological parents to their children

LESSON 1: Math Background: Dealing with Uncertainty

The goal of this unit is to give the students an introduction to the concepts of chance and uncertainty, and to help them to gain familiarity with these concepts as well as learn to handle them in an elementary way.

Many problems in mathematics, just as problems in life, are easier if you put your ideas in order before you attempt to solve the problem. Therefore, in this exercise, students are given practice in organizing as well as collecting and analyzing simple data. They begin by working with number patterns found in everyday situations.

Since the experiences entailed in this exercise involve an element of chance, a complete set of answers cannot be given. Students work in pairs, and are encouraged to make their own predictions based on the observations they have recorded as well as the data they have collected, organized, and analyzed.

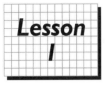

Lesson 1

Math Background: Dealing with Uncertainty

651643
302450
827162

Objectives

- To introduce students to concepts of chance and uncertainty.
- To demonstrate that certain sets of two digits occur with greater frequency than others.
- To be able to give some explanation as to why this occurs.

Skills

- Collecting data
- Organizing data
- Analyzing data

Class Discussion [see below]

Task 1

This activity begins with each student bringing to class the last four digits of his or her social security number. (Students who don't have one can use their parents' or guardians' number.) Each student takes a turn writing his or her number on the chalkboard. Once this has been completed, the teacher explains the terms "first digit" and "last two digits." This is followed by a class discussion as to which digits occur with the least frequency and the greatest frequency. Students have been recording information on a worksheet similar to the one below (figure 9.18), thereby learning how to record this kind of data.

Social Security Worksheet

Digit	Tally	Total
0		
1		
2		
3		
4		
5		
6		
7		
8		
9		

Figure 9.18

This leads to the question, "If I pick a Social Security number and ask you to guess the last digit, what would you guess?" (There is no "right" answer, but the discussion could reveal thoughts students may have about favorite numbers.)

Task 2

Each student chooses a partner, and together they take turns collecting and recording data. The data recorder begins by guessing the sum of the last two digits of an imaginary zip code and writes this guess on a worksheet.

Using the zip code page from a phone book or the post office, the other partner, with eyes closed, randomly points to a zip code number on a page. The data collector then gives the actual sum of the last two digits of the number closest to his or her partner's finger as well as the sum of the last two digits of the next number. This is done for the next 13 consecutively listed numbers, bringing the total to 15 sums in all. The recorder writes each of these sums and counts up and records the number of times his or her guess matched the actual sums.

Some students may make a guess like 28 for the digit sum, but then discover for themselves that the greatest possible sum is 18 (9 + 9). They will probably also discover that sums like 9, 10, and 11 are more likely to occur than numbers like 2 and 17 since many more digit pairs add up to numbers like 10 rather than 2.

Students will alternate jobs as recorder and collector, repeating the experiment at least three more times. Some students begin to get better at guessing as they go from one trial to the next. Some may even be able to explain in the closing class discussion why a guess like 9 is better than a guess like 17.

LESSON 2: Application of Statistics and Probability to the Science of Genetics

In math class the students will learn about the researcher Gregor Mendel and his experiments in the middle of the nineteenth century. The results of those experiments formed the basis of the modern-day science of genetics. Next the students will be introduced to Mendel's detailed methods of organizing and recording this data.

Mendel's work with garden pea plants led him to conclude that plant traits are handed down through hereditary elements we now refer to as genes. He reasoned that each plant receives a pair of genes for each trait, one gene from each of its parents. Based on his experiments, he concluded that if a plant inherits two different genes for a trait, one gene will be dominant and the other recessive. The trait of the dominant gene will appear in the plant. For example, the gene for yellow seeds is dominant and the one for green seeds is recessive. A plant that inherits both of these genes will have yellow seeds (see figure 9.19).

Genetic Probability Models

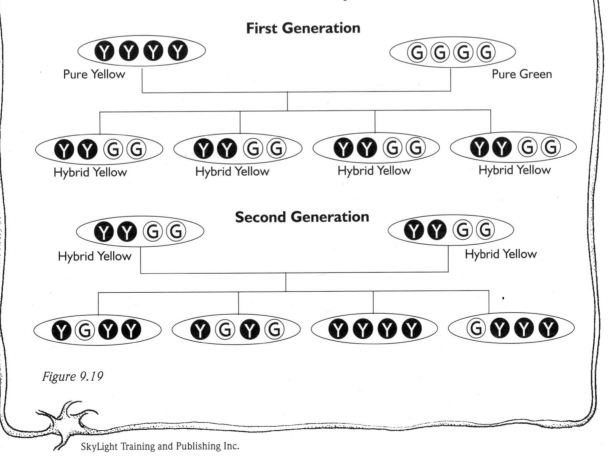

Figure 9.19

The mathematics concepts covered in this lesson are
1. a table of results
2. general probability models
3. probability models for inherited characteristics

Students will predict the probable physical characteristics of offspring (to be done in conjunction with the science unit on reproduction).

The science aspects covered are
1. a background unit on reproduction
2. a discussion on genetic traits and heredity
3. a discussion of Gregor Mendel's use of the scientific method

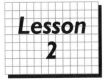

Lesson 2

Application of Statistics and Probability to the Science of Genetics

Objectives
- To help students learn research design and statistics.
- To help students learn design and function of probability models.

Skills
- Estimating
- Multiplication and division

Class Discusssion [see below]

Task 1

Task 1 has two interdisciplinary components: one scientific and the other mathematical. In segment 1, the science and math classes will group together in order to have a larger data base. They are to employ organized and accurate methods of collecting the data (see figure 9.20).

A unit on correlated groups design may be interjected at this juncture. Correlated groups design is a research design in which some of the variance in the dependent variable is caused by a correlation between groups of subjects, or among sets of their scores. The most common form of this research design is a before-and-after study. Begin by giving the entire class a vocabulary test with no preliminary warning. The following week, give half the class a word list to study in school each day.

On the third week, give the entire class a second vocabulary test containing some of the words from the study list. The dependent variable in this case is the score on the second vocabulary test. Many of the differences in the students' scores (the variance) on the second test can be explained by their first test scores. For example, students with very large vocabularies before the experiment would still have large vocabularies after it was over. Thus, regardless of the treatment they receive, the scores of students on the first and second tests almost certainly would be somewhat correlated (probably highly correlated).

In segment 2, students will begin to organize their data from the spelling tests so as to be able to graph their findings.

Genetic Worksheet

		Student	Mother	Father	Siblings
student name	hair color:				
	eye color:				

Figure 9.20

Task 2

Task 2 also has two segments (see figure 9.21). In segment 1, students will "marry" by picking matched numbers out of two baskets (one for girls and another for boys). They will organize and chart their hereditary history, and decide on the number of offspring they will have. Employing Mendel's elementary probability models, they will attempt to predict the probability of the hair and eye color of these offspring. To do this, they must make their own probability models in a clear and easily understood manner.

In segment 2, students with similar hair and eye color combinations will group together in sets of two pairs, and compare their model outcomes to see if any similarities exist. They will then begin to look for any correlations, either positive or negative, to see if any outcomes are predictable. If a correlation is the extent to which two or more things are related to one another, would there be a positive or negative correlation between hair or eye color of parents and their offspring? Why?

Method of Assessment

These new groups of four students will present their findings and conclusions to the class. During the discussion/evaluation period, students in the audience will evaluate whether the data were used in an appropriate manner (see figures 9.22 and 9.23). Were the findings organized so that they made sense, and were the conclusions drawn correct ones? Students must decide if they would have come to the same conclusions. If not, where were the data incorrect? Where was the logic faulty?

PROBLEM LADDER GRAPHIC ORGANIZER

Curriculum Area(s): _Mathematics_   Project Length: _1 to 2 weeks_

Performance Task Title: _How Do Your Genes Fit?_   Grade Level(s): _7–9_

Resources/Materials: _Poster board, markers, colored paper, scissors, glue_

TASK DESCRIPTION

Students will "marry" by picking matched numbers out of two baskets (one for girls and another for boys). They will organize and chart their hereditary history, and decide on the number of offspring they will have. Employing Mendel's elementary probability models, they will attempt to predict the probability of the hair and eye color of these offspring. Students with similar hair and eye color combinations will group together in sets of two pairs, and compare their model outcomes to see if any similarities exist. They will then begin to look for any correlations, either positive or negative, to see if any outcomes are predictable.

PROJECT OBJECTIVES

Student comprehension of concepts

- _research design and statistics_
- _design & function of probability models_

Student skill and process development

- _estimation_
- _multiplication and division_

PRODUCTS AND/OR PERFORMANCES

Group Products

- _"offspring" probability models_
- _group correlation report_

Individual Products

- _correlation group vocabulary_
- _graph_

Extensions

- _probability models for other traits and characteristics_

CRITERIA FOR PRODUCT EVALUATION

Group Products

- _Were the probability models accurate?_
- _Were they easy to understand?_
- _Did the group correlation reports give accurate conclusions?_

Individual Products

- _Were the results accurately displayed?_
- _Were the results easy to understand?_

Extensions

- _Did the new probability models make sense?_
- _Were they accurately displayed and easy to understand?_

Figure 9.21

AUDIENCE STANDARDS FOR GRADING "GENETICS" PRESENTATION

Name:_____ Section:_____ Date:_____

EXCELLENT (E)

___ The presentation was well organized, easy to understand, and contained some interesting and creative insights.

___ Both the science and the mathematics were complete, accurate, and carried beyond the basic requirements for this project.

___ Everyone on the team was well prepared and contributed to the presentation.

___ The presentation had a clear beginning, middle, and end.

SATISFACTORY (S)

___ The presentation seemed adequate, but had nothing especially creative or unique about it.

___ Most of the science and mathematics were accurate.

___ Most of the members contributed something of value.

___ The presentation made sense and held my attention.

UNSATISFACTORY (U)

___ The presentation seemed disorganized and was difficult to understand.

___ The science and/or mathematics were incomplete and/or inaccurate.

___ Not everyone contributed equally.

In four or five complete sentences, explain the reason for the grade you gave.

_____
_____
_____
_____
_____
_____

Figure 9.22

HOW DO YOUR GENES FIT?
Standards for Self-Grading (page 1)

Student self-grading outline for the project "How Do Your Genes Fit?"

Name:_____ Section:_____ Date:_____

How to Grade Your Report
- Report Content and Mathematical Accuracy: Did you answer all the questions completely and correctly? 65%
- Writing Skills: Was the report well written? (Did it have correct spelling and sentence structure?) 25%
- Appearance: Was the report neat and well organized? 10%

How to Grade Your Effort:
The effort grade may be calculated by counting each (E) as 25 points, each (S) as 15 points, and each (U) as 5 points. For example, if there are 2 (E)s and 2 (S)s, the grade will be 80%.

SUPERIOR: (E)
___ My work was superior/excellent.
___ I made many positive contributions to the group effort in every way possible.
___ I encouraged other members and assisted them whenever they needed help.
___ I was key to my group's success.

SATISFACTORY: (S)
___ My work was complete and correct.
___ I made several positive contributions to the group effort.
___ I encouraged at least one group member.
___ I helped my group succeed.

Figure 9.23a

HOW DO YOUR GENES FIT?
Standards for Self-Grading (page 2)

UNSATISFACTORY: (U)

___ I could have done better.

___ I did not encourage others.

___ I did not worry about my group.

___ I kind of goofed off.

In four or five complete sentences, explain the reasons for the grades you gave yourself. Which of your team members were most helpful? Which were least helpful? How were they or weren't they helpful?

Figure 9.23b

SkyLight Training and Publishing Inc.

CHAPTER 10

SECONDARY LEVEL TASKS

Chapter 10 addresses the secondary level. (Because of this, the unit organization differs from that in Chapters 8 and 9.) This chapter contains one unit: "Measurement and Finance: Home Improvement." The unit has two parts: (1) "Painting" and (2) "Flooring," which outlines project extensions.

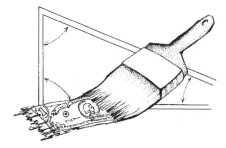

— UNIT ONE —

MEASUREMENT AND FINANCE

Home Improvement

This life skills unit involves the planning and development of a small business. The students are given the hypothetical problem of making bids on several jobs to fix up the first level of the principal's home. They are to research costs and availability of supplies; explore different ways of carrying out the various jobs; take measurements and make calculations for painting, papering, carpeting, etc.; and estimate labor costs. The project extensions provide additional challenges to the students' creative and problem-solving skills.

The unit provides a novel way to increase and strengthen mathematical skills using a hands-on approach. Part 1 deals with making a bid for painting several rooms in the principal's home. The students are charged with putting together an estimate of what their team would charge the principal if he or she were to choose them for the job. The job consists of painting the walls and ceilings of the living room, dining room, and family room.

Part 2 presents some project extensions for this unit, the first one involving an estimate for tiling the bathroom, kitchen, and dining room floors. (Other possible extensions include laying a wood floor in the living room or family room or carpeting that same area.)

SkyLight Training and Publishing Inc.

This unit follows the recommendations suggested by Caine and Caine (1994) for implementation of brain-based learning through the

- provision of variety and stimulation;
- use of product creation and presentation based on topics of student interest;
- use of the group (team) model which allows for individualized learning plans developed according to each student's learning style, assorted intelligences, strengths, interests, and needs;
- use of the community as a resource for supply and labor cost estimates; and
- use of the teacher as a resource, facilitator, coach, and guide.

Following is a list of Caine and Caine's Brain/Mind Learning Principles and how they are implemented in this unit:

1. *The brain is a complex, adaptive system.* Students adapt and learn in a supportive and challenging learning environment. The premise of working at a competitive venture involving calculations for costs of supplies and labor can be a challenge, even for adults. The students, however, can discuss and revise their ideas within their groups and arrive at joint decisions so that the project does not become overwhelming.
2. *The brain is a social brain.* Students learn best by working in small group learning situations.
3. *The search for meaning is innate.* Students work best when they see the relevancy of project objectives.
4. *The search for meaning occurs through "patterning."* Students are made aware of the connections through similarities found in various purchasing and job planning activities.
5. *Emotions are critical to patterning.* It is important that the learning environment be challenging, exciting, and nonthreatening so that learning can be a positive experience. The group environment makes the tasks of evaluating supply costs, labor costs, profit estimates, and measure calculations enjoyable because there is a social quality to the experience.
6. *Every brain simultaneously perceives and creates parts and wholes.* While the students work on individual aspects of the project (costs

and estimations), they can easily keep the "big picture" (the potential cost of a job) in mind.

7. *Learning involves both focused attention and peripheral perception.* While the students are focused on their task, the teacher's as well as the team's attitudes toward the project become part of the learning experience. The team's attitude includes an aspect of socialization, engendering a positive attitude on the part of the students involved.

8. *Learning always involves conscious and unconscious processes.* The students may focus on the finances of purchasing and planning the job, yet their brains will begin to search out similarities in their own everyday environment.

9. *We have at least two ways of organizing memory.* Part of our brain is geared to rote memorization, while another part deals with a spatial/ autobiographical memory that does not need practice or rehearsal, and which allows for instant recall of experiences. This hands-on activity involving measurement, supply-cost research, and development of job estimates is very different from a traditional fill-in-the-worksheet activity, and therefore will be remembered long after their semester has ended.

10. *Learning is developmental.* The more sophisticated the level of student maturity, the greater the sophistication of the project level. The extensions have been suggested as a means of increasing the level of challenge if needed.

11. *Complex learning is enhanced by challenge and inhibited by threat.* Optimal learning occurs through experiences that challenge the intellect, yet are also enjoyable and pose minimal stress. This project provides challenge, yet the group format reduces stress and increases student enjoyment of the challenge.

12. *Every brain is uniquely organized,* and as such, will interpret information and project directions in an individual manner. Individual creativity will result in many unique and original problem solutions for the job bids.

The contextual learning is designed around student interests. All of the learning is structured around real-life issues and problems. The students work together in teams, yet the learning takes place outside the classroom as well as inside. Students have the opportunity to monitor as well as maximize their own learning through metacognitive opportunities for group and self-reflection (see figures 10.3 and 10.4).

Project Objectives

1. *Geometry:* To use calculations for whole as well as partial perimeters and areas in a real-world context.
2. *Measurement:* To improve calculation skills using customary fraction, metric decimal unit, and square-unit measurements.
3. *Money:* To learn to make cost comparisons and purchase-making decisions.
4. *Percent:* To understand and use sales tax calculations with all purchasing in addition to other supply and labor cost estimations.
5. *Time:* To become adept at making calculations using hours and minutes.
6. *Group Dynamics:* To continue fostering teamwork spirit and cooperation among the students.
7. *Self- and Group-Assessment Skills:* To learn and comprehend what "excellent" looks like (rubric instruction and implementation).

Teacher Directions

In order to keep instruction consistent with the goals outlined in the NCTM Curriculum and Evaluation Standards (1989), have students use instruments such as protractors, compasses, architect's scales, triangles, and T-squares to help make hands-on investigations of geometric concepts such as unconventionally shaped areas or perimeters. Calculators are useful in the development and exploration of π and area formulas, and computers serve as an excellent medium for work with vocabulary, lines of symmetry, and congruent figures.

All of these tools and materials help to enhance geometry instruction according to NCTM recommendations; this is not true of traditional paper-and-pencil tests limited to applying isolated formulas to imaginary shapes. For this reason, an end-of-unit evaluation project that has relevancy and captures student interest is recommended, such as this collaborative group project-unit.

Before beginning this project unit, it might be helpful for the students to get an idea of real room size and proportion. As an anticipatory assignment, have the students measure various rooms around the school building, and calculate the square footage of each room. This helps to familiarize each of them with actual room sizes and measurements (making connections).

The students will conduct their work and research in four-member teams. One student can use a meterstick while another uses a yardstick to measure bathrooms, offices, and classrooms. A third student sketches the room and a fourth records and calculates the square metric measurement and footage measurement (with help from team members). Each group posts their sketches and reports their findings to the class.

For help in organizing and presenting this project, use the Problem-Ladder Graphic Organizer (see figure 10.1).

PART 1: Painting

To earn money over the summer, your group has decided to start a house-painting business. Your team's first possible job is to paint several rooms in the principal's home. Your assignment is to put together an estimate of what you would charge the principal if your team were chosen for the job.

You will be painting the living room, dining room, and family room walls and ceilings. All the walls are nine feet high. (See the house floor plan: figure 10.2).

Following are some questions to keep in mind when making up your bid:
1. What will be the square footage of the walls to be painted? (Should window area be included in these calculations? Why or why not?)
2. What will be the square footage of the ceilings?
3. How much paint will each team need if one gallon covers 300 sq. ft.?
4. How much more paint will you need if the principal wants two coats of paint on the walls only?
5. Will your group invest in brushes, rollers, or spray guns? What other supplies will you need to do this job?
6. What will your supplies cost? (Don't forget that every state charges sales tax on the purchase of supplies.) Use newspaper advertisements and store flyers to find the "best deals."
7. If it takes two people 1 hour to paint a 12x12 room with rollers, 3 hours using brushes, and $1/2$ hour using spray guns, how many total

continued on page 187

PROBLEM LADDER GRAPHIC ORGANIZER

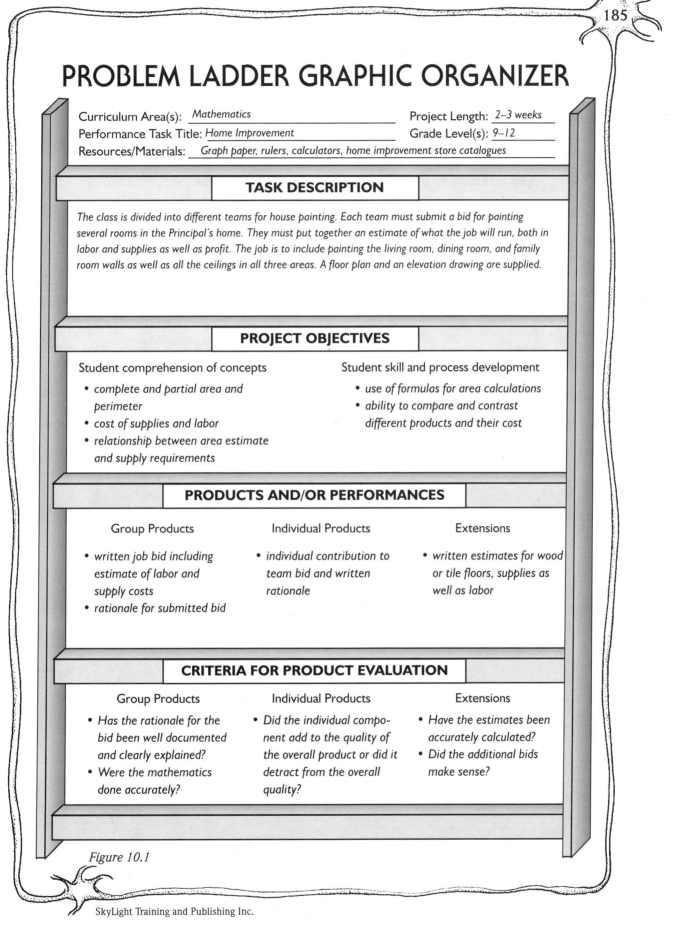

Curriculum Area(s): _Mathematics_
Performance Task Title: _Home Improvement_
Resources/Materials: _Graph paper, rulers, calculators, home improvement store catalogues_

Project Length: _2–3 weeks_
Grade Level(s): _9–12_

TASK DESCRIPTION

The class is divided into different teams for house painting. Each team must submit a bid for painting several rooms in the Principal's home. They must put together an estimate of what the job will run, both in labor and supplies as well as profit. The job is to include painting the living room, dining room, and family room walls as well as all the ceilings in all three areas. A floor plan and an elevation drawing are supplied.

PROJECT OBJECTIVES

Student comprehension of concepts

- complete and partial area and perimeter
- cost of supplies and labor
- relationship between area estimate and supply requirements

Student skill and process development

- use of formulas for area calculations
- ability to compare and contrast different products and their cost

PRODUCTS AND/OR PERFORMANCES

Group Products

- written job bid including estimate of labor and supply costs
- rationale for submitted bid

Individual Products

- individual contribution to team bid and written rationale

Extensions

- written estimates for wood or tile floors, supplies as well as labor

CRITERIA FOR PRODUCT EVALUATION

Group Products

- Has the rationale for the bid been well documented and clearly explained?
- Were the mathematics done accurately?

Individual Products

- Did the individual component add to the quality of the overall product or did it detract from the overall quality?

Extensions

- Have the estimates been accurately calculated?
- Did the additional bids make sense?

Figure 10.1

SkyLight Training and Publishing Inc.

HOUSE FLOOR PLAN

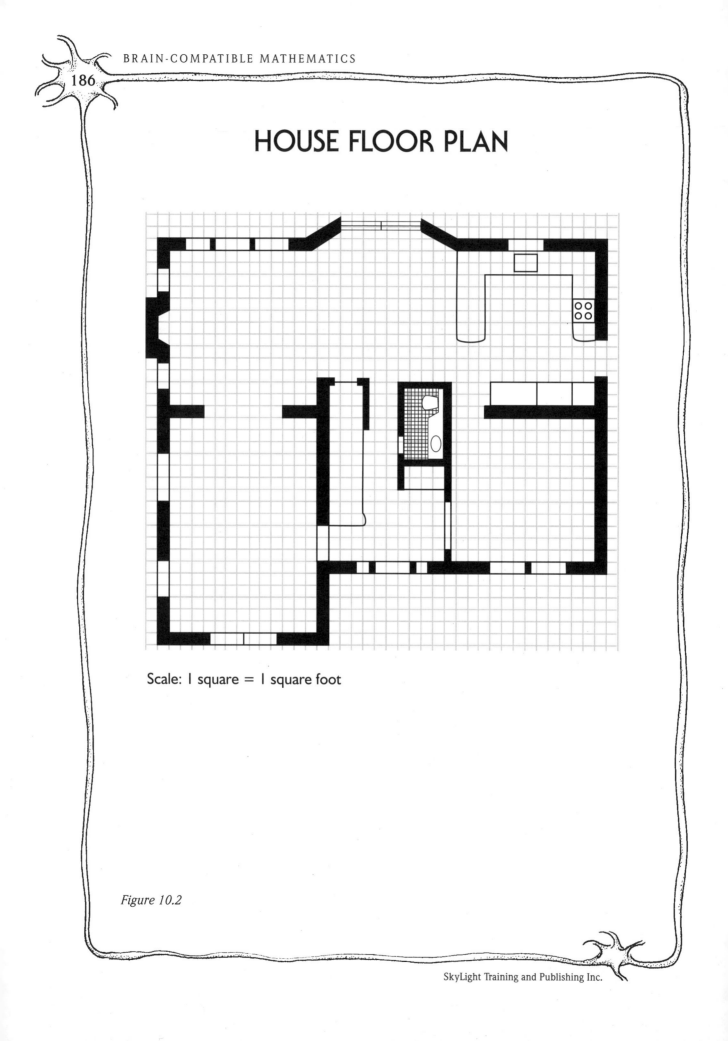

Scale: I square = I square foot

Figure 10.2

hours will it take your team to do the job? How much will charge for labor per person per hour?

8. If your supplies cost _____, and you need _____ hours for the four (or three) of you to do the job, how much will you charge the principal? How much profit do you plan to make?

The results of your bids will be given to the principal, who will choose the most competitive bid.

PART 2: Flooring (Project Extensions)

Your painting job was so successful that the principal also wants to hire you to put in a bid to tile the bathroom and kitchen/dining room floors. The size and cost of the tile and grout are up to you. You can choose any shape or style of tile that you think works well in all the rooms (it can all be the same tile or different tiles). For this job you will need to find out what kind of cement or glue will be needed, its cost, as well as how long it will take to lay the tile. (You must include a written rationale for your labor estimate.)

Another possible extension is putting a wood floor in the living room and/ or family room as opposed to carpeting the same area.

1. What will be the square footage of the floor to be tiled? . . . to be covered in wood? . . . to be carpeted?
2. How much tile glue or cement will be needed if one gallon covers approximately 250 sq. ft.?
3. How much additional wood will you need if the principal wants wood floors in all rooms except the bathroom?
4. What will your supplies cost? (Use newspaper advertisements and store flyers to find the "best deals.")
5. How much will you charge for labor per person per hour?
6. If your supplies cost _____, and you need _____ hours for the four (or three) of you to do the job, how much will you charge the principal? How much profit do you plan to make?

The results of your bids will be given to the principal, who will choose the most competitive bid.

HOME IMPROVEMENT
Evaluation of Group Presentation

Name: _____ Section: _____ Date: _____

EXCELLENT (E)
___ The presentation was well organized, easy to understand, and contained some interesting and creative insights.

___ The mathematics were explained clearly and completely, were accurate, and were carried beyond the basic requirements for this project.

___ Everyone on the team was well prepared and contributed to the presentation.

___ The presentation followed a logical sequence and was easy to follow.

SATISFACTORY (S)
___ The presentation seemed adequate, but was not especially creative or unique.

___ Most of the mathematics were accurate.

___ Most of the members contributed something of value.

___ The presentation made sense and held my attention.

UNSATISFACTORY (U)
___ The presentation seemed disorganized and was difficult to understand and/or follow.

___ The mathematics were incomplete and/or inaccurately done.

___ Not everyone contributed equally.

In a paragraph, explain the reasons you gave the grade you did, and critique the presentation itself.

Figure 10.3

HOME IMPROVEMENT
Standards for Self-Grading (page 1)

Name: _____ Section: _____ Date: _____

How to Grade Your Report

- REPORT CONTENT AND MATHEMATICAL ACCURACY:
  Were all the objectives met? Were the calculations done completely and correctly? Were all the questions answered completely and correctly? Was a valid rationale given for labor costs and project bids? 45%

- WRITING SKILLS & APPEARANCE:
  Was the report well written (did it have correct spelling and sentence structure, was it neat and well organized)? 20%

- CRITIQUE AND REFLECTION: 35%

  Problem Comprehension
  - Can you explain what you had to do for this project?

  Planning of the Strategy
  - Can you explain your strategy for calculating supply and labor costs?
  - How did you organize your information?
  - What was the sequence of steps you followed?

  Executing the Strategy
  - How do you check your work for accuracy?
  - Why did you organize your tables the way that you did?
  - How do you know whether or not what you did is correct?

  Review of the Work
  - Are you sure your answers (bid estimates) are plausible? Why?
  - Could you have found alternative solutions? (How might such a solution look?)
  - What made you decide to use this particular strategy?

Figure 10.4a

HOME IMPROVEMENT
Standards for Self-Grading (page 2)

Mathematical Communication

- Can you explain what you did?
- How would you explain what you did to a teammate who is confused?
- Can you write your own problem using this same strategy?

Mathematical Connections

- Have you ever solved a problem similar to this one? In what ways is it the same? In what ways is it different?

Self-Assessment

- Are these kind of problems easy or hard for you?
- What makes this type of problem easy? What makes it difficult?
- In general, what kinds of problems are especially hard for you? What kinds of problems are easy? Why do you think this is so?

Figure 10.4a

GLOSSARY

assessment. The measuring or judging of the learning and/or performance of students or teachers. *Performance assessments* require students to perform a task that at times may be designed to assess the students' ability to apply knowledge learned in school. *Authentic assessments* are performance assessments that are not artificial or contrived.

authentic learning. Learning about and testing real-life situations (the kinds of problems faced by adult citizens, consumers, and professionals). The learning must have real value and quality. The problems require higher-order thinking skills, and the students know what the expectations are before beginning the work. Authentic learning situations require teamwork, problem-solving skills, and the ability to organize any tasks needed to complete the project, the result of which is an excellent product or performance.

benchmark. A standard or set of standards used for judging the quality of a product or a performance.

brain-based learning. Schooling that relies on recent brain research to support and develop improved teaching strategies. Current research supports the theory that the human brain is constantly searching for meaning, as well as seeking patterns and connections. Strategies that enhance such learning include real-life projects that allow students to use different learning styles and multiple intelligences.

constructivism. An approach to teaching based on research about how people learn. The theory behind this is that each individual "constructs" knowledge for himself or herself, rather than receiving it from others. Constructivist teaching is based on the belief that students learn most effectively when knowledge is gained through exploration and active participation. Students are encouraged to think and explain through the use of broad and connected reasoning rather than the memorization and recitation of facts in isolation.

cooperative learning. A teaching strategy that allows students to acquire social skills as well as knowledge. It combines teamwork with individual and small group accountability. Individuals of varying talents and abilities work in small groups to solve tasks, each group member having his or her own personal responsibility essential for successful task completion.

diversity. A term referring to the recognition of the varied needs of different students. Such needs may include those of ethnicity, language, socioeconomic class, ability levels, disabilities, and gender.

formative evaluation. An evaluation that provides ongoing feedback to determine what students have learned in order to assist in the planning of further instruction. By contrast, *summative evaluation* refers to evaluation used primarily to document the level of student achievement and is given at the end of a unit.

heterogeneous grouping (mixed grouping). The intentional mixing of students of varying talents, abilities, and needs. This encourages the students to learn, assist, and respect one another as individuals.

higher-order thinking skills. Complex reasoning that asks students to go beyond the basic skill of memorizing information. Such skills involve the development of the ability to process information and then apply the information to a variety of situations. Typical higher-order thinking skills are: analyzing, synthesizing, evaluating, comparing, contrasting, generalizing, problem-solving, investigating, experimenting, and creating.

homogeneous grouping (ability grouping). The organization of learners according to their displayed abilities and aptitudes. Also referred to as *tracking.* Such organization is frequently found in school settings where traditional teaching methods (for example, teacher lecture) are also used.

interdisciplinary learning. A philosophy of learning and instruction in which content is drawn from several subject areas to focus on a particular topic or theme. Rather than studying individual subjects in isolation, curriculum areas are organized around a central theme that employs multiple subjects and differing points of view.

multiple intelligences. A theory of intelligence first developed by Howard Gardner, a professor of education at Harvard University, during the mid-1980s. Gardner claimed that our current definition of intelligence must be broader than in the past. He originally identified seven intelligences: linguistic, logical-mathematical, musical, spatial, bodily-kinesthetic, interpersonal, and intrapersonal; he now suggests the existence of several others, including naturalist, spiritual, and existential. All people have every one of the intelligences, but in different proportions.

norm-referenced tests. Standardized tests designed to measure how a student's performance compares with the scores of other students taking the test for statistical norming purposes. Scores on norm-referenced tests are often reported in terms of grade-level equivalencies or percentiles derived from the scores of the original cohort of students.

performance tasks. Activities, projects, or problems that require students to show what they can do. Some performance tasks are designed to have students demonstrate their understanding by applying their knowledge to a particular situation. Performance tasks usually have more than one acceptable solution, and often call for the student to create a response to a problem and then explain or defend the response.

portfolio. A collection of student work chosen to exemplify and document student learning and progress. Portfolios are a valuable way to assess student learning because they include multiple examples of student work and are specifically intended to document progress and growth over time, as well as stimulate student reflection and introspection.

problem-based learning. An approach to curriculum and instruction that involves students in solutions of real-life problems rather than the conventional text-book orientation. This type of instruction begins with a real problem that connects to the student's world. Groups organize their methods and procedures around specifics of the problem, rather than traditional school subjects (similar to authentic learning and interdisciplinary learning). Problems are selected for their appropriateness and the degree to which they illuminate core concepts in the school's curriculum.

rubric. A term used to refer to those specific levels of quality describing a particular performance's appearance. Rubrics are used to evaluate student products and performances that cannot be quantified objectively through the use of traditional percentage and/or numeric standards. Students are given or help to develop the rubric (often with four levels) that describes what they might accomplish through a given product or performance.

REFERENCES

Beyer, B. 1987. *Practical strategies for the teaching of thinking.* Boston: Allyn and Bacon.

Bloom, Benjamin. 1956. *Taxonomy of educational objectives.* New York: David McKay.

The Building Tool Room. 1995. Assessment terminology: A glossary of useful terms. Prepared for "Assessing learning . . . should the tail wag the dog?" Assessing Learning Conference held September 28-30.

Burke, Kay. 1997. *The mindful school: How to assess authentic learning.* Arlington Heights, IL: IRI/SkyLight, Inc.

Caine, R. N., and G. Caine. 1994. *Making connections: Teaching and the human brain.* Don Mills, ON: Addison.

———. 1994. *Mindshifts: A brain-based process for restructuring schools and renewing education.* Tucson, AZ: Zephyr Press.

———. 1997. *Education on the edge of possibility.* Alexandria, VA: ASCD.

Carnegie Council on Adolescent Development. 1996. *Great transitions: Preparing adolescents for a new century.* New York: Carnegie Corporation of New York.

Commission on Standards for School Mathematics of the National Council of Teachers of Mathematics. 1992. *Implementing the K-8 curriculum and evaluation standards.* Reston, VA: National Council of Teachers of Mathematics, Inc.

Costa, A.L., and B. Kallick. 1992. Reassessing Assessment: Seven Issues Facing Renaissance Schools. In *If minds matter: A forward to the future, Volume II,* edited by A. L. Costa, J. A. Bellanca, R. Fogarty. Arlington Heights, IL: IRI/SkyLight, Inc.

Deutsch, M. 1962. Cooperation and Trust: Some Theoretical Notes. In *Nebraska symposium on motivation*, edited by M.R. Jones. Lincoln, NE: University of Nebraska Press.

Doyle, W. 1988. Work in mathematics classes: The context of student's thinking during instruction. *Educational Psychologist* 23 February: 167-80.

Educator in Connecticut's Pomperaug Regional School District 15. 1996. *Performance-Based Learning and Assessment.* Alexandria, VA: ASCD.

Fielding, G., and D. Schalock. 1983. *Integrating Teaching and Testing: A Handbook for High School Teachers.* Eugene, OR: Teaching Research Division, Oregon State System of Higher Education.

Freedman, Robin Lee Harris. 1994. *Open-ended questioning: A handbook for educators.* Menlo Park, CA: Addison-Wesley.

Gardner, Howard. 1983. *Frames of mind: The theory of multiple intelligences.* New York: Basic Books.

———. 1987. Beyond IQ: Education and human development. *Harvard Educational Review* 57(2) May: 187-193.

———. 1991. *The unschooled mind: How children think and how schools should teach.* New York: Basic Books.

———. 1993. *Creating minds.* New York: Basic Books.

———. 1993. *Multiple intelligences: The theory in practice.* New York: Basic Books.

———. 1997. Assessment and instruction in a world of individual differences. Paper presented at the 1997 Association for Supervision and Curriculum Development (ASCD) Conference: Orlando, FL, October.

Goleman, D. 1995. *Emotional intelligence: Why it can matter more than IQ.* New York: Bantam Books.

Guskey, T. 1997. Reporting student learning. Paper presented at the 1997 Association for Supervision and Curriculum Development (ASCD) Conference: Orlando, FL, October.

Hart, L. 1983. *Human brain, human learning.* New York: Basic Books.

Herman, J. L., P. R. Aschbacher, and L. Winters. 1992. *A practical guide to alternative assessment.* Los Angeles, CA: The Regents of the University of California.

Johnson, D. W., and F. Johnson. 1987. *Joining together: Group theory and group skills (3rd ed.).* Englewood Cliffs, NJ: Prentice-Hall.

Johnson, D. W., and R. T. Johnson. 1990. In *Effective teaching: Current research,* edited by Waxman and Walbert. Berkeley, CA: McCutchen.

Johnson, D. W., R. T. Johnson, and E. Holubec. 1988. *Cooperation in the class-room.* Edina, MN: Interaction.

Lambdin, Diana V., Paul E. Kehle, and Ronald V. Preston, eds. 1996. *Emphasis on assessment: Readings from the NCTM's school-based journals.* Reston, VA: The Council.

Lustig, Keith. 1996. *Portfolio assessment: A handbook for middle level educators.* Columbus, OH: National Middle School Association.

Marzano, R. J., D. Pickering, and J. McTighe. 1993. *Assessing student outcomes: Performance assessment using the dimensions of learning model.* Alexandria, VA: ASCD.

McBrien, J. L., and R.S. Brandt. 1997. *The language of learning: A guide to educational terms.* Alexandria, VA: ASCD.

McTighe, J. 1997. Performance-based instruction: Teaching and assessing for understanding. Paper presented at the 1997 Association for Supervision and Curriculum Development (ASCD) Conference: Orlando, FL, October.

———. 1997. What happens between assessments? *Educational Leadership* December 1996/January 1997: 7-12.

McTighe, J., and G. Wiggins. 1997. Understanding by design. Paper presented at the 1997 Association for Supervision and Curriculum Development (ASCD) Conference: Orlando, FL, October.

National Center for Educational Statistics Third International Mathematics and Science Study. 1998. *Pursuing excellence: A study of U.S. fourth, eighth, and twelfth grade mathematics and science achievement in international context.* Washington, DC.

National Council of Teachers of Mathematics. 1989. *Curriculum and evaluation standards for school mathematics.* Reston, VA: NCTM.

————. 1991. Professional Standards for Teaching Mathematics. Reston, VA: NCTM.

————. 1995. *Assessment standards for school mathematics.* Reston, VA: The Council.

National Middle School Association. 1995. *This we believe: Developmentally responsive middle level schools.* Columbus, OH: National Middle School Association.

O'Keefe, J., and L. Nadel. 1978. *The hippocampus as a cognitive map.* Oxford: Claredon Press.

Palmer, Jackie. 1993. *Improving science and mathematics education/A tool kit for professional developers alternative assessment.* Portland, OR: Northwest Regional Educational Laboratory.

Perkins, D. 1992. *Smart schools: From training memories to educating minds.* New York: The Free Press.

————. 1995. *Outsmarting IQ: The emerging science of learnable intelligence.* New York: The Free Press.

Perkins, D., and G. Salomon. 1988. Teaching for transfer. *Educational Leadership* 46(1) September: 22-32.

Polya, G. 1988. *How to solve it: A new aspect of mathematical method.* Princeton, NJ: Princeton University Press.

Pressley, M., and J. Dennis-Rounds. 1980. Transfer of a mnemonic keyword strategy at two age levels. *Journal of Educational Psychology* 72: 575-582.

Pressley, M., J. R. Levin, and H. D. Delaney. 1982. The mnemonic keyword method. *Review of Educational Research* 52: 61-91.

Resnick, L. 1987. *Education and learning to think.* National Academy Press, Washington, DC.

Slavin, R. 1981. Synthesis of research on cooperative learning. *Educational Leadership* (May): 655-58.

198

Stenmark, Jean Kerr, ed. 1989. *Assessment alternatives in mathematics: An overview of assessment techniques that promote learning.* Berkeley, CA: The California Mathematics Council.

———. 1991. *Mathematics assessment: Myths, models, good questions, and practical suggestions.* Reston, VA: National Council of Teachers of Mathematics.

Stiggins, R. J. 1994. *Student-centered classroom assessment.* New York: Macmillan.

Sylwester, R. 1995. *A Celebration of neurons: An educator's guide to the human brain.* Alexandria, VA: Association for Supervision and Curriculum Development.

Van Patten, J., Chun-I Chao, and C. Reigeluth. 1986. A review of strategies for sequencing and synthesizing instruction. *Review of Educational Research* 56: 437–471.

Webb, Norman L., Arthur F. Coxford, eds. 1993. *Assessment in the mathematics classroom: 1993 yearbook.* Reston, VA: National Council of Teachers of Mathematics.

Wolf, Dennie Palmer, Paul G. LeMahieu, and JoAnne Eresh. 1992. Good measure: Assessment as a tool for educational reform. *Educational Leadership* 49 (8) May: 8-11.

INDEX

There are
one-story intellects,
two-story intellects, and three-story
intellects with skylights. All fact collectors, who
have no aim beyond their facts, are one-story minds. Two-story minds
compare, reason, generalize, using the labors of the fact collectors
as well as their own. Three-story minds idealize, imagine,
predict—their best illumination comes from
above, through the skylight.
—*Oliver Wendell*
Holmes

SkyLight
PROFESSIONAL DEVELOPMENT

We Prepare Your Teachers Today for the Classrooms of Tomorrow

Learn from Our Books and from Our Authors!

Ignite Learning in Your School or District.

SkyLight's team of classroom-experienced consultants can help you foster systemic change for increased student achievement.

Professional development is a process not an event. SkyLight's experienced practitioners drive the creation of our on-site professional development programs, graduate courses, research-based publications, interactive video courses, teacher-friendly training materials, and online resources—call SkyLight Professional Development today.

SkyLight specializes in three professional development areas.

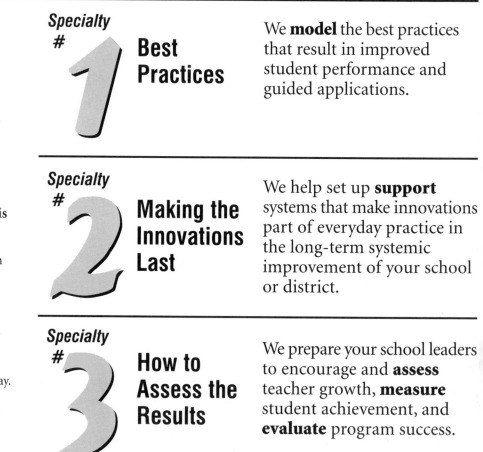

Specialty # 1 Best Practices

We **model** the best practices that result in improved student performance and guided applications.

Specialty # 2 Making the Innovations Last

We help set up **support** systems that make innovations part of everyday practice in the long-term systemic improvement of your school or district.

Specialty # 3 How to Assess the Results

We prepare your school leaders to encourage and **assess** teacher growth, **measure** student achievement, and **evaluate** program success.

Contact the SkyLight team and begin a process toward long-term results.

SkyLight
Professional
Development

2626 S. Clearbrook Dr., Arlington Heights, IL 60005
800-348-4474 • 847-290-6600 • FAX 847-290-6609
info@skylightedu.com • www.skylightedu.com